THE ART OF
OPTIMISM

THE ART OF
OPTIMISM

YOUR **COMPETITIVE** EDGE

JIM STOVALL

© Copyright 2018 – Jim Stovall. All rights reserved.

This book is protected by the copyright laws of the United States of America. This book may not be copied or reprinted for commercial gain or profit. The use of short quotations or occasional page copying for personal or group study is permitted and encouraged. Permission will be granted upon request. For permissions requests, write to the publisher, addressed "Attention: Permissions Coordinator," at the address below.

SOUND WISDOM
P.O. Box 310
Shippensburg, PA 17257-0310

For more information on publishing and distribution rights, call 717-530-2122 or info@soundwisdom.com

Quantity Sales. Special discounts are available on quantity purchases by corporations, associations, and others. For details, contact the Sales Department at Sound Wisdom.

While efforts have been made to verify information contained in this publication, neither the author nor the publisher assumes any responsibility for errors, inaccuracies, or omissions.

While this publication is chock-full of useful, practical information; it is not intended to be legal or accounting advice. All readers are advised to seek competent lawyers and accountants to follow laws and regulations that may apply to specific situations.

The reader of this publication assumes responsibility for the use of the information. The author and publisher assume no responsibility or liability whatsoever on the behalf of the reader of this publication.

ISBN 13: 978-1-64095-021-4
ISBN 10: 1-64095-021-4
ISBN 13 eBook: 978-1-64095-022-1
ISBN 13 TP: 978-1-64095-023-8
ISBN 10 TP: 1-64095-023-0

For Worldwide Distribution, Printed in the U.S.A.

Cover design by Eileen Rockwell
Interior design by Terry Clifton

1 2 3 4 5 6 7 8 / 21 20 19 18

CONTENTS

CHAPTER ONE

REINTRODUCING OPTIMISM

"A pessimist sees the difficulty in every opportunity; an optimist sees the opportunity in every difficulty."
—Winston Churchill

As you read these words, I want you to know that I am greatly honored. I realize that you have many choices in how you spend your time and money, so I'm grateful you have chosen to let me and my message through this book become a part of your life.

As a young man, I never intended to be a writer and wasn't even a reader. When I could read with my eyes as you are doing within the pages of this book or on the screen of an electronic device, I don't know that I ever read a whole book cover to cover. My pursuits were much more focused in the arena of athletics as opposed to academics.

After losing my sight in my 20s and living the last 30 years as a blind person, I have averaged reading a book a day thanks to audio books and high-speed digital players. Becoming a reader made it possible for me to become a writer and has opened so many other doors in my world. I'm hopeful and expectant that this book will do the same for you.

Having read thousands of books, I realize some books are entertaining, others are informational, and a few are literally transformational. I am dedicated to the proposition that this book and the act of infusing optimism into your life will become transformational for you and everyone around you. To this end, any time the message of this book seems distant or hard to apply in your life, you can contact me directly via Jim@JimStovall.com.

For over 20 years, I have written a syndicated weekly column known as *Winners' Wisdom,* which appears in countless newspapers, magazines, and online publications all around the globe. When you send me your questions or challenges via email, feel free to request the weekly *Winners' Wisdom* column, and it will be sent to you every Thursday, at no charge, as my ongoing commitment to your journey of optimism.

For several years, I have done a weekly national radio show every Monday. I also do a local radio program in my hometown, which is hosted by my friend and colleague Pat Campbell. Pat is fond of saying, "He who controls the definitions controls the debate." I believe this is true in world politics, late-breaking news events, and how you and I structure our lives as we move toward success.

I have reviewed a number of dictionaries, and among the most common definitions of optimism is "a predisposition or tendency to look on the more favorable side of events or conditions." If you study a bit deeper into the definitions and origins of the terms *predisposition* and *tendency,* you will find that in the modern vernacular these terms denote something that is already set in place or prearranged.

While elements of your physical self such as being tall, having blue eyes, or being left-handed may be predetermined by genetics, I maintain and am committed to the concept throughout this book that whether you are an optimist or a pessimist is totally in your control and may well be the most important decision you will ever make in your personal or professional life.

I have written over 40 books to date and have been a part of seven of them, thus far, becoming movies. I have written over 1,000 columns, made countless speeches for millions of people, and have appeared on a myriad of TV and radio shows discussing all manner of topics. I firmly believe that the journey of exploration you and I are taking within this book to explore optimism and how it impacts us may well be the most important topic I have ever tackled.

In a famous Supreme Court decision involving pornography, one of the justices declared, "I don't know if I can define it, but I know it when I see it." While you may have never thought about the precise definitions of the words *optimist* or *pessimist*, those words undoubtedly evoke images of people from your past who you think of as optimistic or pessimistic.

Zig Ziglar was a great friend and colleague of mine. He impacted my life as well as the lives of millions of people around the world. His legacy of influence will continue through his books, videos, and audios for centuries to come. Zig often said, "I'm an optimist. I would go after Moby Dick in a rowboat and take the tartar sauce with me." I knew Zig for over two decades, and I never saw him in a bad mood or portraying any emotion other than absolute optimism.

When I began speaking at large corporate and arena events where a number of speakers were booked onto the same program throughout the day, I crossed paths with Zig Ziglar many times. You would be surprised how often the backstage preparations for positive-thinking rallies and motivational events are far from positive or motivational.

I remember one particular day when the crew setting up an event had not been allowed into the arena at the time called for in the contract. There were an inordinate number of difficulties with the lighting, sound system, and computer setup backstage. Just as the frustration, confusion, and utter chaos reached a boiling point, Zig Ziglar arrived backstage and proclaimed to everyone within shouting distance, "It's great to be here, and this is going to be an amazing day!"

One of the overworked, over-stressed technicians turned to Zig and said quite sarcastically, "Well, you're sure in a good mood today."

Without skipping a beat, Zig smiled broadly and declared, "Yes, sir. I'm in a great mood today because over 20 years ago, I decided to be in a great mood today."

That encounter has stayed with me for many years and began my thinking about and study of optimism, which has culminated in this book.

I read dozens of personal development books each year. One of the most fascinating titles in recent memory is Malcolm Gladwell's book *The Tipping Point*. In his book, Mr. Gladwell shows how small ideas, thoughts, or trends can become wildly popular and morph into something that impacts society as a whole. If you read *The Tipping Point*, like me, you will be convinced that the concept is valid, and tipping points occur. The question you may be left with, as I am, is: Can we create, influence, or encourage a tipping point? If so, that power or ability becomes a tremendous tool. If not, it is little more than an interesting phenomenon to observe much like the weather or the orbit of the planets.

Within this book, you will be convinced not only of the power of optimism but also of your ability to control it in every area of your life.

Socrates lived in Greece almost 2,500 years ago. He was a revolutionary teacher and philosopher. The true impact of someone's life's work can only be fully examined in hindsight; and as one of my favorite authors, Louis L'Amour, often said, "No person can be judged except against the backdrop of the time and place in which they lived."

Socrates' teachings were quite profound, but when you understand that his work became the basis for the teachings of Plato, Aristotle, and all other great thought leaders who came after him, it becomes clear that Socrates was transformational. His concept now known as the Socratic Method—a series of questions and answers that evoke self-discovery—is the foundation of what we now know as a university education.

In many of my arena and corporate speeches, I stand on the shoulders of Socrates as I encourage and create a sense of expectation with my audience as I implore them, "Please do not miss the power of this message due to the weakness of the messenger. I am not someone who has arrived at his destiny, but instead, I am a fellow traveler on the road to success. I do not have the answers you are seeking, but I do have some questions that will be the framework for our time together, and you will discover that you already have the answers you seek."

Among Socrates' most profound ideas was his statement, "An unexamined life is not worth living." It is easy for us to reflect upon the news of the day and everything going on around us, but rarely—if ever—do we delve into that last great frontier inside our own minds, spirits, and souls to examine: *Who are we, where are we going, and what do we stand for?*

Our thoughts control our actions, and our actions result in the way we live our lives. As I always tell my audiences in corporate and arena events, "You can change your life when you change your mind." A key missing element in the process of changing our mind is to examine the lens through which we view the world. We can never overcome the images we see through the lens, but through a process my friend and colleague Dr. Stephen Covey called a paradigm shift, we can change lenses. Optimists and pessimists can live in the same environment and encounter the same situations, but their individual lenses offer them each a completely different reality.

I'm reminded of the two shoe salesmen who lived and worked during the beginning of the 20th century. These two salesmen worked for the same company, and the company had decided to open a new market for their shoes in the South Pacific Islands. The president of the shoe company called the two salesmen into his office and informed them they were both being transferred to a remote South Pacific island. The first salesman we will call Oscar the Optimist enthusiastically proclaimed, "What a great opportunity and wonderful adventure to get to move to a tropical island and sell our shoes." The second salesman we will call Peter the Pessimist muttered, "You've got to be kidding! I can't believe they expect us to move to some backward island in the middle of nowhere and try to do business."

In the coming days, Oscar and Peter made preparations for the big move. Oscar whistled while he worked, told all his friends and family he would be sending them wonderful cards and letters, and he eagerly awaited the departure date for his voyage to the South Pacific. Peter was dejected and depressed. He delayed making any arrangements or preparations for the move until the last minute and then finally, in frustration, he threw a few belongings into a bag and rushed to the port to catch the boat for his dreaded departure.

As the great ocean liner's horn sounded indicating they were leaving the dock for the three-week journey halfway around the world, Oscar and Peter settled into their cabins. Oscar found his accommodations to be efficient, convenient, and excitedly rustic. Peter found his identical cabin to be cramped, uncomfortable, and primitive.

During the 20-plus-day voyage, Oscar toured the entire ship and learned many new things about sailing and navigation. He met a number of interesting people onboard, some of whom became his lifelong friends, and he wrote notes and postcards to friends and family back home describing his wonderful voyage and big adventure.

Peter remained mostly in his cabin throughout the entire voyage and only ventured out for meals. He avoided other passengers and all the onboard activities. His only interaction with the ship's crew was to lodge a number of complaints about the ship, the food, and the weather.

After more than three weeks at sea, the ship arrived at the South Pacific island where Oscar and Peter would begin their new careers and their new lives. As the two salesmen walked down the gangplank from the ship to the dock, Oscar was refreshed, invigorated, and filled with great anticipation. Peter was exhausted, disoriented, and filled with dread.

As Oscar and Peter strolled into the port city, they discussed how they would divide up their new sales territory, which was made up of the one tropical island where they had just arrived. Peter groaned, "I'm not going one inch farther. I'll take this end of the island, and you can have the other side." Oscar readily agreed, thinking it would give him a chance to explore the entire area and find a suitable place to live and work on the other side of the island.

Peter the Pessimist shuffled down the street and entered the first dockside rooming house he could find. It was dirty and rundown, but it was what he expected so he agreed to rent a small apartment on the ground floor. He closed the shutters, drew the drapes, put out the Do Not Disturb sign, and went to bed thinking: *I need to take a couple of weeks off to recuperate from that interminable trip before I begin trying to sell shoes in this ridiculous God-forsaken place.*

As Oscar the Optimist left his colleague Peter, he looked around the port city with great excitement, taking in all the exotic sights, sounds, and smells of his new home.

Oscar caught a train to the far end of the island and sat in a window seat so he could enjoy all the scenic views of this marvelous tropical island that he had been blessed to be assigned to.

While he thought he might be tired after the long train ride, Oscar found himself to be surprisingly rested and refreshed as he looked over the town at the other end of the island where he would work and make his new home. Oscar enthusiastically toured the area, meeting as many of the inhabitants of the town as he could. After all, they were going to be his new neighbors, and he was ecstatic that everyone was so helpful and friendly. After considering all his many options, Oscar rented a seaside cottage that had a breathtaking view of the coastline and offered a ringside seat to savor the amazing sunsets over the ocean each evening.

While Peter listlessly lounged around his gloomy and cluttered apartment, Oscar energetically set up housekeeping in his new seaside home and arranged to host a party so he could meet all his new neighbors. Peter avoided all the residents of his apartment building as he was certain they were all thieves and ne'er-do-wells while Oscar discovered that his neighbors were some of the most fascinating people he had ever met.

Some of Oscar's new neighbors were world travelers who, after experiencing every environ around the globe, decided to settle on this particular tropical island while other neighbors were native to the island and saw no reason to leave paradise for anything else that might be across the ocean.

Peter's dread increased and his negative attitude grew throughout his two-week self-imposed vacation before he planned to start work. Oscar used the occasion of his party to begin introducing new friends and neighbors to his line of shoes that he was very proud to be bringing to the island.

Oscar felt no reason to take any time off as he enjoyed his job and never really felt like he was working. After all, he thought, it's only a matter of sharing these great shoes with new friends and neighbors who he was convinced would be as excited about his products as he was.

Peter and Oscar could not have had more different views, impressions, or opinions of their new island home and worksite, but they both discovered one thing immediately that they could agree on. Virtually all the native inhabitants of the South Sea island where they had been sent were barefoot. It seemed that no one wore shoes.

Barely a month after Oscar and Peter had their meeting with the president of the shoe company, they both sent a telegram back to the home office. Peter the Pessimist's telegram read, "To Whom it May or May Not Concern: Finally arrived in this dirty, impoverished, out-of-the-way place and discovered that no one here even wears shoes; therefore, I am sending back all inventory and will be returning on the next ship that will get me out of this place."

Oscar's telegram to the office of the shoe company read, "Greetings from Paradise. I am both thankful and grateful that you sent me here. It's like being able to live in a tropical resort and pursue my profession at the same time. Just when I thought it couldn't get any better, I discovered the most amazing thing. No one on this island wears shoes. It's a completely untapped market. Please send all available shoe inventory to this island as soon as possible as I am convinced this will be the most outstanding market for our shoes we have ever experienced."

Oscar and Peter experienced the same conditions and environment. All factors were identical, but their perceptions and their results were polar opposites. The only difference between ecstatic success and abject failure was that Oscar was an optimist, and Peter was a pessimist. Neither one of them could have changed their job assignment, travel arrangements, or any of the conditions on the island, but each of them had within their power to change their outlook, and that alone made a world of difference.

As a blind person myself, I have a keen understanding of the concept that bad things can happen to good people. As I tell my audiences when I speak, however, my blindness is no more or less significant than someone else's divorce, bankruptcy, illness, or unemployment. We are all only as big as the smallest thing it takes to divert us from our higher calling and destiny.

Many pessimists do not even believe in the concept of optimism much less their own ability to convert to a better way of thinking and living, but just as if they didn't believe in gravity, it still exists and influences every element of their lives every day. Sometimes those who do not believe in optimism can come to an understanding of its existence by recognizing and understanding the power of pessimism.

Often the best way to understand the impact of light is to recognize and experience darkness.

CHAPTER TWO

THE POWER OF PESSIMISM

"No one is smart enough to be a pessimist."
—PAUL HARVEY

always hate to be the one to have to tell my readers, my audience, or any individual I may be talking with the cold, hard facts of life, but the reality is that life isn't fair. This life we're living right now is great, grand, and wonderful, but it isn't fair.

Here in America, we pride ourselves on opportunity and equality. These are precious principles worth living for and, in the case of some brave patriots, even worth dying for, but equality doesn't guarantee us a place at the finish line. Equality guarantees us a place at the starting line. From there we can go as high and far as we choose as long as we understand that life still isn't fair.

I've enjoyed the privilege of having seven of my books, to date, turned into movies. I will never forget when my first novel, *The Ultimate Gift*, was made into a major motion picture from 20th Century Fox starring James Garner, Brian Dennehy, and Abigail Breslin.

I have had the opportunity to be very involved with each of the film projects based on my books. In fact, if you go to see one of my movies, be sure to look for a brief scene with a limo driver, or in one case a bartender, because that's me. Like Alfred Hitchcock, I've always enjoyed showing up somewhere on the silver screen in all the films based on my novels. You wouldn't be the first to see the irony in the blind guy playing the limo driver, but I can assure you no one has been killed or even seriously injured on the set of any of our movies.

Another aspect of the film projects I have enjoyed working on has been the music. Our soundtracks have included Bob Dylan, Patsy Cline, the great American composer Aaron Copland, and one of my all-time favorites B.B. King.

I remember the first time I saw B. B. King in concert. He was a great showman and a great musical artist. One of the lyrics that stuck with me said, "If it wasn't for bad luck, I wouldn't have no luck at all."

At first, this would definitely seem to be a negative statement; however, there are many people going through life with that lyric as their perception. As we learned from the shoe salesmen, the facts can't be altered, but our reality can be totally revised based on our outlook.

Adolf Hitler is often credited with saying, "If you tell a lie long enough and loud enough, it becomes reality."

It is important as you judge your own perceptions and attitudes with respect to optimism and pessimism that you observe what I call Stovall's 11th Commandment. This homemade commandment of mine states, "Thou shalt not kid thyself." This is my version of Mr. Shakespeare's immortal words, "To thine own self be true." The biggest and most damaging lies we ever tell are those we tell ourselves and then share with the world.

As a blind person myself, I'm always intrigued and fascinated by how sighted people navigate. If you go to a huge shopping mall, you will find large maps strategically placed throughout the entire facility. All of these maps are identical with one key exception. This is the simple phrase and arrow designating "You are here." You can be familiar with every square inch of a giant shopping mall and be unable to navigate anywhere until you know the exact spot where you are currently located. In much the same way, we must have an honest and accurate assessment of our own perceptions of the world that make us an optimist or a pessimist.

Often, we don't have a choice about what happens to us in our lives, but we always have a choice in what we're going to think about it and do about it. For every person you can find who has been devastated by a setback in their personal or professional life, I can show you someone else with the same circumstances who has used that potential setback as a springboard to greater things.

Every personal development or success author of the last 100 years, including me, has drawn upon the work of Napoleon Hill. I have been privileged to work with Don Green, head of The Napoleon Hill Foundation, on several book projects, which have included my own work and that of the late, great Dr. Hill. Much as we discovered in the last chapter that Socrates introduced original thoughts and concepts, Napoleon Hill opened the vault of wisdom through his seminal book *Think and Grow Rich*. *Think and Grow Rich* was published in 1937 and remains the bestselling book in its field to the present day.

Among other priceless nuggets of wisdom, Napoleon Hill said, "Every adversity, every failure, every heartache carries with it the seed of an equal or greater benefit." Hill would have been the first to also say that every adversity contains the seed of total failure and devastation. The choice is ours.

Often, optimists are accused of being like Pollyanna or an ostrich that buries its head in the sand ignoring the reality of real-world problems. I believe true optimists are realists. They acknowledge the problem but are committed to continuing to seek the benefit or opportunity within. In much the same way, I think most pessimists fail to be realists as they only look for, recognize, and accept the worst result in every situation.

Most people can look back at their own past and remember situations that were devastating at the time but, with the benefit of hindsight now, can be viewed in a positive light. This is certainly true in my life.

It may have been the worst single day of my life. I had been diagnosed in my late teens with a condition that would eventually result in my blindness. Throughout my 20s, my sight did, indeed, fade and dim, and then there was the morning at age 29 when I awoke and realized the remainder of my sight was gone.

I rushed into the bathroom, turned on the light, and stared at where I knew the mirror was hanging over the sink, but there was, quite simply, nothing there. The dreaded diagnosis had become reality, and I began the adjustment of learning to live my life as a blind person. I was 29 years old, I had never met a blind person, and I did not have a clue what I was going to do with the rest of my life.

The only plan I could come up with that fateful morning involved moving into a little 9- by 12-foot room in the back of my house. In my little room, I gathered my radio, my telephone, and my tape recorder, which comprised my whole world. I really fully intended to never walk out of that 9- by 12-foot room again.

The mere thought of my life today running a television network, writing over 40 books with seven of them to date turned into movies, speaking to millions of people around the world in arena events, or writing my weekly syndicated column would have seemed as foreign to me as going to the moon. I couldn't have imagined it, so I simply sat in my 9- by 12-foot self-imposed prison, day after day, getting more depressed and more discouraged.

I am convinced I would still be in that same room 30 years later except for a choice I made between the two options that presented themselves to me.

After several months experiencing the frustration and terror of being a totally blind person, a visitor came to my little room. He introduced himself and told me he was from the state government agency that worked with blind people. He proceeded to give me a white cane and tell me all the limitations I would experience in my future. I told him of my desire to still find a way to have a career and make some kind of living. He emphatically proclaimed the words I remember as if it were today. "Look, you're just not getting it. You're never going to work or have a job like other people. You're not going to be able to support yourself, and you won't have normal friendships or relationships like everyone else. Men won't respect you, women won't like you, and children will be afraid of you. The sooner you accept this reality, the better off you'll be."

His statement represented the first option that was presented to me. The second option came in the form of an audio cassette tape given to me by a neighbor. A little old lady who lived on the corner of my street told me that this message might help me and left the tape behind as she said goodbye.

The tape was a speech given by Dr. Denis Waitley. I had never heard of Dr. Waitley at that time but found out he had been a Blue Angel pilot, was a highly-respected psychologist who had worked with the U.S. Olympic Team as well as returning prisoners of war, and he had written the bestselling book *The Psychology of Winning*.

In his speech, Dr. Waitley spoke of a world of possibilities and then closed his presentation by reciting his epic poem entitled "If You Think You Can, You Can." Every stanza of Dr. Waitley's wonderful poetry repeated "If you think you can, you can. If you think you can, you can." I wore out that cassette tape, bought another, and eventually got Dr. Waitley's recording in a digital format that I still have to this day.

So there I was sitting in my little 9- by 12-foot self-imposed prison with a white cane propped up against the wall to the left of me and a tape recorder repeating Dr. Waitley's emphatic statement, "If you think you can, you can" to the right of me. I didn't know at that time which message was right and which message was wrong, but I eventually knew in my heart and said aloud, "Someone is lying to me."

Years later as I was signing books after an arena speech, I was confronted again by the same state government worker who had come to my little room. He was somewhat embarrassed, and I reassured him that he should not feel bad as he had been one of the great inspirations of my life.

When pessimists deliver their bad news, they're not really lying to you. They are lying to themselves and telling you what they believe to be the truth. I chose to believe Dr. Denis Waitley then and now, and it has made all the difference.

I was honored to have Dr. Waitley write the foreword to my first book, and over the years we have shared the stage together many times. On the occasion of his 80th birthday, he came to one of my speaking engagements, and in spite of his protests I brought him on stage, introduced him to the audience, and presented him with my own version of a lifetime achievement award symbolized by that same white cane I had been given many years before when I chose his message and what it represented instead of the message that the white cane represented. As I handed Dr. Waitley the cane, he told me and my audience that to commemorate his 80th birthday, he was planning to climb Mount Kilimanjaro in Africa, and he was going to take my white cane and plant it at the summit; and then he, without any preparation or warning, recited from memory his epic poem "If You Think You Can, You Can."

Choosing Dr. Waitley's message did not represent the finish line in my life. It was merely the starting line for my great race.

One of the discoveries and decisions I made at that point in my life that has been instrumental in getting me from there to here is that I don't take advice from anyone who doesn't have what I want or who hasn't been where I want to go. My grandfather often said, "A man with experience doesn't have to take a backseat to a man with a theory."

I knew I had to limit the pessimistic white cane input in my life. Please understand that today I know many accomplished and successful blind people. A lot of them use a white cane masterfully and have wonderful mobility skills. When I refer to a white cane in this context, I am simply describing the negative message that I rejected so I could accept Dr. Waitley's powerful and positive message.

Even after making the transformational decision to be an optimist and believe that "If you think you can, you can," I still was stuck all day, every day in my 9- by 12-foot room; however, I began to change my world.

As I described in the last chapter, I had never been a reader, but sitting in my little room in the back of my house, I began to devour audiobooks. If you look at the lifestyle characteristics among Fortune 500 CEOs or self-made millionaires, you will find that reading is the activity that most of them share in common.

As I listened to book after book, I was hoping to find someone in my situation or even a worse circumstance who overcame it and triumphed. I was frustrated until I read a book about Nelson Mandela. I had never heard of him, but through the audiobook I discovered that he was imprisoned in an 8- by 7-foot cell, which ironically I calculated to be approximately half the size of my little room; but he emerged with strength of character and love in his heart to become the president of his country. I mentally added the voice of Mandela to that of Dr. Waitley as I continued to read and study.

It was months later on the monumental day when I finally decided to walk out of my little 9- by 12-foot room that had been my domain since losing my sight. The first day I emerged from my self-imposed prison, I didn't start a business, or make millions of dollars, or get a gold medal, or write a bestselling book, or receive an Emmy award; but instead, I walked approximately 52 feet to my mailbox. I have been privileged to be a part of many accomplishments and much success throughout my life, but that 52-foot trek down my driveway to my mailbox beside the street may be my highest achievement.

As I slowly shuffled my way down the driveway, scared to death and drenched in sweat, I imagined Nelson Mandela walking beside me, and I literally heard Denis Waitley's voice in my head repeating, "If you think you can, you can. If you think you can, you can…." Eventually, I stretched out my arm, and my hand brushed against the mailbox at the curb. I had arrived at my long-anticipated destination.

As I stood there, my foot touched the curb at the edge of my street, and even though I had lived in that house for over a decade as a sighted person, I discovered something that moment as a totally blind individual that I had never known before. I realized, for the first time, that I lived on a magical street, because I fully understood that the street that it had taken me months to even attempt to walk to was connected with another street which intersected with another street which would take me anywhere in the world that I wanted to go.

It did, it has, and it still does; but the important thing for you to realize as you read these words is the fact that you live on a magical street, and although I don't know your name or your address, I can assure you, my dear reader, that your street is magical and will, without fail, take you anywhere you want to go. The journey from where you are to your ultimate destiny begins in the time and place where you find yourself at this moment.

As I slowly made the transformation back into the real world beyond my 9- by 12-foot little room, I communicated with other blind people who assured me that the two biggest obstacles about being blind were the inability to read and the inability to drive.

One of the books I had read during my exile in my little room was by Dr. Robert Schuller who subsequently became my friend, mentor, and colleague. Dr. Schuller provided a humbling endorsement for the cover of my very first book. In his book, he wrote, "Never get the 'how are you going to do it' mixed up in 'what are you going to do.'" Using Dr. Schuller's logic, I realized I didn't want to read words on a page with my eyes or drive a car myself. I understood that

I simply wanted to consume books and travel everywhere I wanted to go.

As I have mentioned previously, thanks to high-speed audiobooks, I don't know anyone who has read more books than I have; and thanks to limousines, first-class seats on airlines, and my assistants, I have literally traveled several million miles since leaving my little room. We must focus on where we want to go, not how we're going to get there, and we must focus on what we want to get done and not how we're going to do it.

The message "If you think you can, you can" is true and has proven reliable throughout every challenge in my personal and professional life, but I have to accept the fact that while I can do it, it may get done differently from the way other people do it. In fact, as we will explore in a subsequent chapter, opportunity comes disguised as a problem, and great opportunities come disguised as great problems.

This has certainly been the case in my life and will prove true for you if, when you find yourself at that great intersection that presents the two roads known as optimism and pessimism, you take the road less traveled and live your life as an optimist.

CHAPTER THREE

BORN OPTIMISTS

*"There are only two ways to live your life.
One is as though nothing is a miracle. The
other is as though everything is a miracle."*
—ALBERT EINSTEIN

firmly believe that optimism is our natural state, and we have to learn to be pessimists. I believe we are all born optimists.

There are only two basic things that scare babies. These are loud noises and falling. Both should create concern for parents and babies. As we become more aware of the world around us, we are taught fear, limitations, and disappointment. Each of these emotions gives rise to pessimism.

If you can imagine an arena filled with 10,000 business-people when I go onstage and ask for volunteers to come forward and sing a song, do a dance, or paint a picture, how many volunteers do you think we might have? Certainly no more than a handful. Now if you'll change one slight element in the illustration, and instead of 10,000 business-people make it 10,000 kindergartners, how many do you think would be willing to come forward? If you thought virtually all of them, you and I are in agreement.

We are born thinking we know how to do things, and the possibilities are limitless. Then we are taught we don't have the talent, skill, background, or education to do what we want to do. This innate sense of born optimism was taught to me by a special young man who remains among the most influential people in my life as I believe he will be in yours.

I am often asked by reporters which person I have met has impacted my life the most. This is not an easy question, because through my work in movies, television, and writing books as well as my syndicated columns, I have met A-list actors, world champion athletes, political leaders, and elite businesspeople around the world. All of them have impacted me. I have thought a lot about it, however, and there is one special individual who has had a lasting impact on me. Ironically, I met him before I knew anything about optimism.

As a young man, I had one singular goal and focus in my life, and that was to be an All-American football player and make my living in the NFL. Shortly after I learned of my impending blindness, I decided to continue with my plans to attend a local university even though I couldn't play football. Near that university, there was a school for blind children, and I'm not sure if my motives were to learn more about blindness, make some kind of bargain with God, or just to help out, but in any event, I went to the school for blind children and met the principal.

I told her that I was a college freshman, and I had no background, training, or experience working with blind kids, and I would like to teach in her school. You can imagine how excited she was to see me! But, she was a kind soul and told me that if I really wanted to teach there, they had one child I could work with one-on-one.

I agreed, and she explained that Christopher was four years old, was totally blind, and had many other physical problems. Following their many tests, they had determined that Christopher would never develop or advance any more than he already had. And what they wanted me to do was keep him quiet and keep him away from the other kids so they could learn their lessons.

As I look back on it today, I realize that Christopher was suffering from the most severe disability of all—that is, being faced with no expectations. We always live up to the expectations that we have of ourselves or those expectations that we allow other people to place upon us. Optimism is merely an expectation of greatness while pessimism is an expectation of failure.

They had no expectations for Christopher, and the only training they gave me in order to work with him were two very simple things. First, they instructed me to keep his shoes tied, as they were afraid he would trip and fall because he had never learned to tie his shoelaces. Second, they told me I had to keep him away from the stairs because he had never learned to climb the stairs, and they were afraid he would fall down the staircase.

Other than those two things, they really didn't care what I did as long as I kept Christopher quiet so that the other students could learn their lessons.

That first day, I was introduced to Christopher and immediately noticed that he was, indeed, totally blind and much smaller than you would expect a four-year-old child to be. He had many other emotional and physical problems.

He and I sat down and had a serious conversation, and I told him, "Young man, before I leave here, no matter how many weeks or months or even years it takes, you are at least going to learn how to tie your shoes and climb the stairs."

And he replied, "No, I can't."

And I responded, "Yes, you can."

And he replied, "No, I can't."

And I responded, "Yes, you can."

And he replied, "No, I can't…"

If you have ever spent any length of time with a four-year-old child, you know that they can argue like this all day long.

Christopher and I began working every day, learning how to tie his shoes and climb the stairs. Meanwhile, I was attending the university and facing what I thought were insurmountable obstacles. I couldn't see well enough to get around anymore and couldn't read the textbooks.

When it got difficult, I simply prepared to quit.

I went to the school for blind children for what I thought would be my last day. I met with the principal and told her that because of my own visual impairment and impending blindness I was going to have to drop out of college, so I wouldn't be able to come there and work with Christopher anymore because I simply couldn't make it.

I didn't realize that Christopher had been dropped off early that morning, and he was standing outside the open door to the office overhearing our entire conversation. So, as I went out to tell him goodbye and tell him that I loved him and tell him that I hoped that someday someone else would show up and spend some time with him, he turned to me and optimistically repeated my own words back at me by saying, "Yes, you can!"

And I replied, "No, I can't."

And he persisted, "Yes you can!"

And as I replied, "No, I can't" once again, I was mentally preparing an explanation so I could justify to Christopher how my challenges were somehow different or greater than his were. But, before I could begin my weak explanation, it hit me like a ton of bricks. The obvious answer was, "Stovall, either get up and do something with your life, or quit lying to this poor kid in telling him he can do things in his life."

Three years later, I graduated from that university with honors. And the same week, I had the privilege of my life, with what little vision I had left, to observe then-seven-year-old Christopher climb three flights of stairs, turn and sit on the top step, and tie both of his shoes.

About six weeks after the miraculous day when Christopher climbed the stairs and tied his shoes, he died of a brain tumor. The tumor was the condition that had caused him to lose his sight in the first place, and eventually it took his life.

As I was attending his funeral, one of the other teachers said to me, "Isn't it a shame we'll never know how much he could have developed or contributed had he been given a full life?"

I told her that he had already made his contribution because anything I did from that point forward, I would owe to him.

They tell me that I have shared Christopher's story with over a million people, live in events around the world, and now I am sharing it with you through this book. Many of those people—and hopefully you—will use Christopher's example as a platform to examine your dreams, take possession of them, remove the obstacles, eliminate the excuses, and realize that any dream you have inside of you is well within your capacity to achieve.

When Christopher died, it was almost as if he had a will. He left me three separate things that I want to pass on to you.

First, Christopher left me with the certain knowledge that there is no such thing as an insignificant person. If God had ever created an insignificant person, it would have been Christopher. His whole biography would read, "Christopher lived to be seven years old. He learned how to tie his shoes and climb the stairs." These were all of the accomplishments that Christopher could claim after his brief life, but he has changed the lives of thousands of people around the world through his example of courage.

Second, Christopher left me with the certain knowledge that there is no such thing as an insignificant relationship. All relationships are critical. Each of them is important. There are people in your world who are struggling. They're trying to decide whether their dreams can come true.

And finally, Christopher left me with the certain knowledge that there is no such thing as an insignificant day, because when we live our lives in the present, every day of the rest of our lives holds within it your key to greatness, which is your ability to build on your past and create your future by living out your destiny today and learning valuable lessons that can be implemented in your life.

Only through teaching Christopher to tie his shoes and climb the stairs could I have ever learned the profound, impactful, and life-changing lessons he taught me, and through me and my books, columns, and speeches, he has now taught the world.

To this day, whenever I am faced with a challenge or obstacle and find myself leaning toward pessimism, I simply imagine trying to explain my weak excuses to Christopher—my ever-present ambassador of optimism—and the path ahead toward greatness seems clear.

Just as I believe we are all born optimists and it is our natural state, I also believe that the world around us presses in upon us with pessimism as we age and grow. We are confronted with literally thousands of messages each day from other people, the media, and countless online sources. Most of these myriad of messages are frightening, negative, and promote pessimism.

It's important to remember news is not normal. In a brief newscast or scan of the newspaper headlines, you will find all manner of violence, criminal activity, and disasters. The overwhelming majority of events that happen on any given day are positive and would promote optimism. If the media reported on reality instead of obscure, isolated events, the headlines would tell of good people who got up this morning, took care of their families, went to work, and did a great job all day. This is the real world we live in, but it doesn't sell newspapers.

Just as we are constantly pushed toward pessimism, we seem to be able to find ways to be outwardly optimistic. Our natural state is to have our mood and internal attitudes reflected in our behavior. Kids act this out every day while adults think and feel one way on the inside but too often act another way on the outside.

I am reminded of the story about the small Midwestern town during the tremendous drought in the 1930s now known as the Dust Bowl. The drought was so intense and extended for so long that the citizens of this particular town decided to all come together and pray for rain.

At the appointed hour, all the townspeople and farmers from the surrounding area gathered at the town square and began to pray for rain. I'm certain they told themselves and would have told anyone who asked that they fervently believed their prayers would be answered and the rain would come.

As if on cue at the conclusion of the community prayer meeting, the sky opened up, and it began to rain. The mayor of the town and all the leading citizens of the area as well as the minister began to cheer wildly and dance in the street amidst the downpour.

One nine-year-old little girl who had been the only child at the prayer meeting calmly held up her umbrella, popped it open, and casually walked home as she had been convinced all along that her prayers would be answered and the rain would come. As we look back on this scene, we realize that the adults gave lip service to optimism, but one little girl showed them all how to act and live as an optimist.

One of the great privileges of my work in movies, television, writing, and speaking is to have been able to meet and form relationships with some of the greatest people of the 20th and now the 21st century.

I will never forget the day that I was working in my office when the phone on my desk buzzed. The woman who screens our calls let me know that John Wooden was on the phone and wanted to speak with me. Well, I was initially ecstatic as I had grown up as a fan and followed the string of championships that Coach John Wooden and his UCLA Bruins amassed over a decade. John Wooden and his teams rewrote the record book, and most sports experts agree that his record for total number of national championships may never be broken.

My excitement waned as I realized John Wooden is a fairly common name, and there may be thousands of people with the same name. When I asked our receptionist if it was "the" John Wooden, she assured me it was because he wanted me to sign some books for Kareem Abdul-Jabbar and Bill Walton among others.

I was privileged to get to talk with Coach Wooden that day and many more days over the next several years. He passed away a few months shy of his 100th birthday and was sharp, wise, and a powerful influence on me and countless other people around the world until the day he died. Coach Wooden taught me that we can hold on to attitudes, beliefs, and habits that suit our goals and release the ones that don't.

John Wooden grew up on a farm during the early days of the 20th century. One day as he and his brother were working in the barn, his brother played a practical joke on him which culminated with Coach Wooden expressing his displeasure by using some profanity just as their father walked into the barn.

Coach Wooden told me that his father sat him down and calmly told him that words are what we use to express who we are and what we stand for. His father then asked young John Wooden to promise to never use profanity again. Coach Wooden gave his word to his father, and as he told me that story 90 years later, he proudly proclaimed, "Jim, from that day to this I have never once used profanity."

You may be thinking, as I did, how outrageously impossible that seems, but once I got to know Coach Wooden as a colleague, mentor, and friend, I understood that it was just a part of his character.

He told me about one of his national championship games in which his players seemed somewhat unfocused and listless. Coach explained there are times when, to get a team to pull together and become fully engaged, it is an advantage for a head coach to actually get a technical foul on purpose.

Coach Wooden stepped onto the basketball court and approached the referee saying, "Sir, I realize there's a word I can say right now that will result in you calling a technical foul on me. I know the word to say, and I'm very familiar with it, but many years ago I promised my father I wouldn't use profanity, so I'm just hoping you can give me a technical foul without my having to say the word."

Coach Wooden went on to describe how the referee did, indeed, give him a technical foul. In the huddle, he told his players that he hadn't said or done anything wrong. They fiercely pulled together, outplayed their opponent significantly in the final few minutes of the game, and won that national championship.

We have control of the attitudes, the habits, and the optimism we need in order to achieve everything we want in this life. It's a matter of controlling our attitudes and not letting them control us.

As we have explored earlier, our expectations or the expectations that we allow other people to place upon us control our destiny. Just as we control our attitudes and performance, those around us can exert a tremendous influence on our attitudes, actions, and outcomes.

I'm reminded of the young teacher who was assigned to teach a class of failing students in a troubled school. The principal and the school administration had given up on these students and decided to just put them all in one class to minimize the negative impact on the rest of the school and dump them on the new young teacher. She enthusiastically began treating the kids in her classroom with respect and high expectations. The previously failing students began performing up to her expectations, and by the end of the semester, their grades were higher than any of the other classes in the school.

When the principal called the young teacher into his office and asked how she had performed this academic miracle, she confidently explained, "Well, sir, when I was assigned to the class, I pulled all of their files and checked out their records. I was surprised to discover that these failing students had IQs ranging from 110 up to 138, and since I knew they had above-average intelligence, I pushed them academically, and they performed as would be expected."

The astonished principal laughed heartily and informed the young teacher, "Those numbers weren't their IQ scores. They were their locker numbers."

The young teacher and her class leave us all with a powerful, enduring lesson. When the dream is big enough, the facts don't count. Optimism can overcome financial problems, physical disabilities, personal challenges, as well as bad grades.

CHAPTER FOUR

WHY BE AN OPTIMIST?

*"Positive thinking will let you do everything
better than negative thinking will."*
—ZIG ZIGLAR

In this chapter, we are going to explore a number of reasons why you should be an optimist. Optimism will positively impact every aspect of your daily life, but beyond the health, wealth, and success outcomes, there's one overarching reason you and I should be optimists. It's a better way to live.

We always find what we're looking for, and if we expect a great day, we will have a great day. If we expect a great week, we will have a great week, and if we expect a great year, we will have a great year. This, inevitably, results in us having a great life and being able to share it with colleagues, friends, and loved ones around us.

I have a colleague and friend in the writing and speaking business. He has a home on the beach in Florida where he spends each winter. Each year, snowbirds en masse descend upon his area and rent condominiums around him for the season.

He told me about one impactful morning he spent sitting on his deck drinking coffee. As he was enjoying the sights, sounds, and smells of the ocean and the beach that stretched out before him, an elderly lady approached on the sidewalk below his deck.

She greeted him warmly, told him she would be his neighbor for the season, and asked, "I am new here, and I want to know about the other people who live around here. Can you tell me about the neighbors?"

My friend asked her, "What are the people like where you come from?"

She enthusiastically responded, "Well, I'm from a rural area in the Midwest where everyone is friendly, outgoing, and will do anything for their neighbors. Everyone there is more like family than anything else."

My friend nodded and assured her, "You'll find the people around here to be just like that."

A few moments later, a gentleman approached my friend sitting on the deck and called, "Good morning. I'm new around here. Can you tell me what the people in the area are like?"

My friend, once again, asked, "What are people like where you come from?"

The man responded gruffly, "I'm from the East Coast. I live in a port city where people are rude, mean, and nasty. It's a dog-eat-dog world up there."

My friend nodded understandingly and stated, "Well, you'll find people around here to be just like that."

If you expect to have a great meeting, a wonderful meal, an entertaining show, a memorable vacation, or a successful career, you won't be disappointed. On the other hand, if you expect gloom, doom, and failure, you won't be disappointed. Optimism works like a universal form of room service. You simply order up what you want, and it will be delivered to you in the style, portion, and condition you expect. Why would we ever expect anything less, and why wouldn't we always be optimistic?

If you're one of those skeptical souls who needs concrete, measurable, and specific reasons to be an optimist, you won't be disappointed. There are more than enough facts, statistics, and evidence to satisfy you. Optimism is your secret weapon. It is custom-designed specifically for you, and it is capable of bringing you everything you want. No one can take optimism from you.

In his emotional and profound book *Man's Search for Meaning*, Dr. Viktor Frankl described being a successful professional with a flourishing career, nice home, and wonderful family during the late 1930s in Austria. Then, in a short period of time, the Nazis invaded and destroyed his business, took his home, and imprisoned or killed all of his family. He found himself being tortured in a concentration camp. As Dr. Frankl vividly described the circumstances and conditions, I could not imagine a more helpless and hopeless situation.

In the midst of the horrific reality, Dr. Frankl discovered that while the Nazis could take his home, business, family, and his very life, they couldn't take away his optimism and positive attitude. In the midst of pain, hatred, and death, he could feel and express love, hope, and optimism. He went on in his book to describe how optimistic prisoners of war remained more healthy, happy, and able to survive the ordeal, while pessimistic prisoners seemed to suffer and die.

Dr. Frankl used his experience gained in the most tragic and horrible situation imaginable to create many new theories and techniques known as Logo Therapy in psychology and behavioral science that are still used to improve lives and lift the human condition over 75 years later.

Dr. Frankl vividly demonstrated that no one can take our optimism from us, but unfortunately we too often disarm our own secret weapon and take the optimism we own away from our daily lives and the situations where it can make all the difference.

I heard a story about some Irish immigrants coming to America at the end of the 19th century. They scrimped and saved all their money for several years just to buy the cheapest tickets on a ship headed for America. While the ocean liner offered a number of luxury cabins, this Irish family was forced to sleep below decks in the most uncomfortable accommodations known as steerage.

The Irish father and mother had packed as much food as they could for them and their children to eat during their voyage to America, but due to significant headwinds, the trip took longer than expected, and they ran out of food.

As the father huddled below the deck watching his family slowly starving to death, he was tortured by the fact that he could see between the planks that made up the deck right above his head and could observe a sumptuous banquet being served to the first-class passengers barely out of his and his family's reach. He and his family were starving to death right below the most delectable and abundant array of food imaginable.

Finally, in desperation, the father crept up the stairs and asked one of the ship's stewards if he could get a few crumbs or leftovers for his starving family. The steward was alarmed and replied, "Sir, while your sleeping accommodations are below deck in steerage, these nightly banquets are prepared for all of our passengers including you and your family."

Without optimism, you can starve to death in the midst of a banquet, live an impoverished life in the midst of wealth, or be depressed and miserable in the midst of a joyous celebration. We are the only ones who can keep the power of optimism from giving us everything we want in our lives.

If you're still in need of reasons to become an optimist, try this. Being an optimist has been scientifically proven to improve your life, health, and longevity.

In a study, university researchers quantified all the aspects of optimism so they could measure its effects. They found that living your life as an optimist could improve your longevity by 19 percent. To put this into perspective, nonsmokers' longevity is improved 5-10 percent as opposed to those who regularly smoke tobacco; therefore, we can conclude that being a pessimist is twice as detrimental to your health as smoking cigarettes.

In a test conducted on a cross section of women for risk factors associated with atherosclerosis, it was determined that—over a three-year test period—optimistic women experienced no detrimental health effects from thickening arteries while pessimistic women experienced symptoms of atherosclerosis and impaired arteries.

If you're already healthy, optimism will help to keep you healthy. Clinical research has shown that being optimistic will boost your immune system. In a cross section of patients given a flu vaccine, it was determined that three weeks after the vaccination, optimistic patients had much higher positive antibody counts than pessimistic patients. These antibodies that optimists have in significantly higher quantities than pessimists are the key to avoiding illness, disease, and aging.

No less than five separate medical studies on the correlation between optimism and HIV disease progression concluded that optimistic HIV patients remain healthier, live longer, and respond better to treatment.

In his fascinating book *The Anatomy of an Illness*, Dr. Norman Cousins recounts his own struggle with arthritis and heart disease. A research scientist himself, Dr. Cousins got a ringside seat to observe the power of optimism as he saw it work in his own body. He believed that our attitudes and outlook could physically change antibodies and endorphins within our systems that could help to avoid or even cure disease.

In addition to the hospital-prescribed treatments for his diseases, Dr. Cousins prescribed himself an ongoing therapeutic regimen of *Candid Camera* TV shows and Marx Brothers movies. Optimism does, indeed, improve our wellbeing, and you can laugh your way toward health.

Optimists don't just enjoy better health. They enjoy more success and wealth.

I met Steve Forbes in early 2000, shortly after I had been honored by the President's Committee on Equal Opportunity as the Entrepreneur of the Year. Mr. Forbes was compiling a book entitled *Forbes Great Success Stories: Twelve Tales of Victory Wrested from Defeat.* That book featured my journey from poverty to prosperity along with eleven other business and financial superstars.

Working on that book was the genesis of my ongoing friendship with Mr. Forbes. Whenever I'm in New York, he and I try to carve out a morning or an afternoon so we can sit in the library in the Forbes Building and discuss all manner of topics including business, politics, and success. Steve Forbes is a great mentor and friend as well as being the standard bearer for capitalism and free enterprise in America and around the world.

Forbes magazine and Forbes media represent great resources to study and understand the science of wealth and success. Mr. Forbes leans heavily on real-world experience as opposed to theories about wealth and success.

Research into why optimists make better business leaders was reported by Forbes. The research revealed that entrepreneurs are more likely to be optimists than pessimists. This is important as the vast majority of new jobs and new wealth come from small business. Optimists are more likely to start their own business as they see the possibilities and don't focus on the problems. Pessimists are more likely to read the negative business headlines and use reports of unemployment, inflation, or instability as excuses to not launch their own enterprise. Whenever you see a big business, you can rest assured it began as a small business and was started by an optimist.

Optimists in business are better communicators. None of us can succeed on our own. We have to utilize the efforts, ideas, and ingenuity of others. In order to get other people to believe in your dream, you have to be an optimist. People want to embrace optimists and follow them while they want to avoid and ignore pessimists.

When employees or colleagues are confronted with negative thoughts, conditions, or news reports, optimists can step in and immediately turn the tide by finding the opportunity beyond the clutter and noise.

Optimists see the big picture and look far into the future. All of us are subject to a psychological influence known as the recency effect. The recency effect causes the latest or most recent occurrences to be dominant in our mind, attitude, and outlook. Optimists have the ability to look beyond short-term setbacks, downturns, or recent economic reversals while pessimists assume these negative conditions to be permanent.

Great baseball pitchers display characteristics of optimism and shake off the impact of recency. If an optimistic pitcher gives up a homerun, he is likely to see it as a one-time occurrence and simply ignore it as he bears down on the next pitch. When a pessimist gives up a homerun, he confronts the next batter and assumes it's going to happen again, which is more likely to occur because he believes it. This is true in business as well as baseball.

Optimists in business have a tendency to utilize a characteristic that Napoleon Hill described as going the extra mile. Optimists will always outwork and outperform pessimists because they believe in an eventual victory and know their efforts will be rewarded. When an entrepreneur or business leader displays these optimistic efforts, his or her colleagues and employees are most likely to follow suit. This concept becomes readily apparent during sporting events in which one player on the field, through his own effort, can turn the tide of a game or even the whole season.

Optimists are more likely to read, study, and take self-improvement courses because they firmly believe the new information and inspiration will propel them to even greater success in the future. Pessimists reject career-building or self-improvement resources as they don't believe them to be relevant, valid, or effective.

Optimists make better investors and get higher results because they believe the opportunity is out there, and they simply need to find it. There's a big difference between someone who is convinced something exists, is readily available, and waiting to be found and someone who is unsure whether that which they seek is even in existence.

Optimists in business set out to locate and collect the opportunities they are convinced are there. Pessimists are trying to decide whether success is even possible and, if so, where it might be hiding.

Now that we know scientifically and verifiably that optimism can make us healthy, wealthy, and happy, the task is left to us to unleash this force in our own lives. It's easy to believe dreams come true for others, but only optimists are convinced that their dreams are readily available and waiting to be captured.

Being an author is generally a singular and solitary pursuit. You can have millions of your books sold around the world, but as a rule most authors never get any feedback from their readers. Many years ago, I determined to be an exception to this rule and give out my contact information in every one of my books. As I stated earlier, you can join the group of readers around the globe who connect with me via Jim@JimStovall.com.

One of the amazing surprises I received was when one of my more illustrious readers, the legendary golfer Jack Nicklaus, wrote me a handwritten note after reading one of my books. This started our ongoing correspondence and communication that I treasure to this day. I have learned much from Jack Nicklaus—a lot of it before I knew him personally.

In the spring of 1986, Jack Nicklaus was competing in The Masters golf tournament, which is held each year at the gorgeous Augusta National Golf Course. The week of the tournament was established to coincide with when the azaleas bloom. There cannot be a more magnificent setting anywhere for four days of the greatest competition golf in the world.

The fact that Jack Nicklaus was playing in The Masters was nothing unusual as he had won that prestigious tournament five times before, which was more Masters championships than anyone else had amassed. The unusual aspect of that Masters tournament in 1986 was the fact that

Jack Nicklaus was 46 years old, had made the cut after the first two days to continue playing throughout the weekend, and was near the top of the leaderboard in the final round. It was unthinkable that someone 46 years old could win The Masters, but Jack Nicklaus was and still is a man used to doing the unthinkable.

Growing up, I always enjoyed watching golf tournaments on television with my father. In 1986, I was 28 years old and almost totally blind. In fact, that particular tournament would be the last championship I ever got to watch on television.

I remember sitting less than a foot from the TV and squinting at the blurry images as I tried to watch my hero, Jack Nicklaus, do the impossible. At the beginning of the round, the announcers, pundits, and experts all commented on the novelty of the old guy still being in the tournament. In the middle of the round, a few speculations about the unbelievable possibility of Jack Nicklaus actually winning began to creep into the commentary. By the last few holes of the tournament, all the announcers along with everyone in the massive gallery at the Augusta National course and countless millions of people around the world watching on TV were convinced they were observing history being made.

I remember the dim and blurry images of Jack Nicklaus crouching down behind his golf ball and squinting at the subtle undulations of the manicured green trying to determine which way his critical putt would break. His son Jackie was caddying for him that day and was trying to help his father read the green. Only later was it revealed that Mr.

Nicklaus was struggling with his own eyesight—certainly not to the extent I was but more than enough to make it difficult for him to make out the subtle variations on the Augusta National's pristine greens.

Eventually, he stood, grasped his putter, and assumed his familiar stance over the ball. Just as the tension seemed to reach a crescendo, Mr. Nicklaus stepped away from the ball and walked around the green for a moment seeming to view the putt from several angles. Finally, he stood over his golf ball again, drew his putter back, and confidently stroked the ball into the middle of the cup, winning his sixth Masters championship at an age when most golfers are hanging it up or getting ready for the Seniors Tour.

Only when I got to know Mr. Nicklaus personally did I fully understand and appreciate what occurred during that critical moment of the championship that day. As Mr. Nicklaus explained, he never hit a golf shot unless he had visualized himself making the perfect swing resulting in the ball going exactly where he wanted it to be. He pointed out that while he didn't always hit a perfect shot, it worked the vast majority of the time. Any student of golf would have to admit that Mr. Nicklaus's visualization technique—which is nothing more than optimistically previewing his performance—worked exceedingly well and caused him to be the most successful golfer to ever play the game throughout his career.

If we are going to live a great life and create the personal and professional success we seek, we don't need to blaze a new trail. We just need to follow the examples of

Jack Nicklaus and other great optimists who are winning in every area of life.

CHAPTER FIVE

MEET THE OPTIMISTS

"Things turn out best for those who make
the best of the way things turn out."
—COACH JOHN WOODEN

f you want to climb to the top of a mountain, don't ask someone climbing on the path beside you about the best way to reach the summit. Ask someone who is descending from the top after successfully climbing the mountain. Success is an exercise in following the leader. Optimists see the best in great people and emulate their successful habits and techniques.

In my work on television, in the movies, on arena stages, and in compiling my books, I have met, interviewed, and worked with some of the most successful people from all walks of life. Many of their stories are recounted in my book *Ultimate Hindsight*. Optimistic people's stories in their own words and their success will reinforce that optimism is the best way to live and succeed.

I had the privilege of meeting and working with Louis Gossett, Jr. when my book *The Lamp* was turned into a movie. Writing lines for an Academy Award-winning actor like Mr. Gossett is a great thrill, privilege, and responsibility.

The Lamp book and movie story involves a couple frustratingly living out their pessimistic lives of quiet desperation. They acquire a dubious garage-sale lamp that brings a genie-like character, portrayed by Louis Gossett Jr., into their lives. He offers them three wishes of anything they ever wanted that they couldn't get on their own. After much deliberation, they determine they want a million dollars, great jobs, and a happy marriage but discover that these goals and anything else they ever wanted were always totally within their reach. It is a classic tale of going from pessimism where nothing is possible to optimism where everything is possible merely through a shift in attitude and perception.

Mr. Gossett was everything I hoped he would be and more. He embodied the message of *The Lamp* movie and was kind and gracious to all of us who worked with him on the set.

Louis Gossett, Jr. has enjoyed an incredible movie career, and long after most people have retired, he is still busy making films. At this stage in his career, he told me he is most interested in movie parts that help him express his faith and his philosophies on living a successful life.

When I asked him to share more of his optimistic thoughts, he spoke candidly and directly.

> "The worst resentment that anybody can have is one you feel justified to keep. I am dedicating the last of my life to an all-out conscientious offensive against racism. Violence is a war, and I would pray that the energy we exert on war gets reverted back to a communal effort to save the planet. So perhaps in my own small way I can generate some energy toward the salvation of the planet because when we win a war, we win a dying planet.

"I think what's more important than law is the hearts of the people. We need to do whatever it takes to get our children together and pay attention to them because that's our future. What's in the hearts and minds of our children is what's in our future.

"We all have a bout with death and things that touch our mortality. When that happens, all that bling-bling gets thrown away because all you've got is you and God. The Lord may not come when you want Him, but he's always going to be there on time. I'm cancer-free. I'm on antioxidants and acupuncture and a different diet, and I have a different outlook on life. I don't have resentment any more. It's wonderful."

Louis Gossett has become a good friend and mentor to me. He has often shared with me stories about being raised by his great grandmother who was born a slave. He has seen hatred and love as well as failure and success, and through it all, Lou Gossett has been the soul of grace, dignity, and optimism, which has made him a star on the big screen and a true success in life.

Dan Marino has been inducted into the NFL Hall of Fame. Sports fans and pundits often while away the hours arguing who was the best of all time. Any such debate or conversation about quarterbacks has to include the name Dan Marino.

He was drafted into the NFL in 1983 in what has been known as the "quarterback class." There were many great college quarterbacks entering the NFL that year, and Dan Marino was the last one selected in the first round. He went on to lead his Miami Dolphins to the playoffs 10 out of his 17 seasons in the NFL.

Like most great optimists I have met, when asked about his advice on life, Dan spent most of his time talking about other people and good causes including our Narrative Television Network and very little time talking about himself.

Optimists freely give their time and money because they believe in abundance and remain confident that their future will continue to bring them all they want for themselves and the people and causes they care about.

> "As you know, I focus my efforts to provide programs and services for children, teens, and young adults with autism and other special needs. The Dan Marino Foundation, established in 1992, has grown, and the Dan Marino Center receives over 50,000 visits annually. In addition, we opened the doors in October 2013 for Marino Campus, an educational and recreational facility for young adults ages 18 to 26 years old.

> "We know that the good work and contributions made through the Narrative Television Network will continue to enhance the lives of so many people. In June, I was the keynote speaker

at the Family Café in Orlando with over 6,000 in attendance, and my message there would be one that can certainly be shared: 'Don't ever let anyone tell you that you can't do something. You have to do the work, but don't listen to anyone who says you can't.'"

All quarterbacks lead their teams while on the field. Dan Marino can lead us all as we pursue an optimistic and successful life.

Lee Iacocca has been voted among the top 20 business executives of all time. He has the distinction of developing the Ford Mustang and the Chrysler minivan. Both vehicles permanently altered the industry.

Optimists are people who believe in invention, innovation, and new possibilities. I wrote to Mr. Iacocca asking him to share some of his optimism with me and my readers. You will see in his comments below he has a true passion for automobiles and the business arena.

"Your letter arrived at a most opportune moment since someone walked into my home and the subject was about the passion in what a person chooses to do with their life. This is a good place to start. I believe if a person follows their passion, they will ultimately be a success. And sticking to a career path is a good way to achieve this.

"In my autobiography, I write, 'When the chips were down, my mother found nothing wrong with working in the silk mills so I could have lunch money for school. She did what she had to do. When I got to Chrysler, I found a royal mess, but I did what I had to do.' What we can take from this is no job is too menial, and all work has value. Sometimes a person needs to make difficult decisions for the greater good.

"Giving back, no matter what a person's personal circumstances, is one of the best ways to reap the rewards of living in this wonderful country. I say in my book *Where Have All The Leaders Gone?*, 'Each of us has to put something back in. Let's start a dialogue about public service. The point is very simple: There is no free lunch. For everything you get, you have to give something back.'

"These two principles are so important to have a good life, and I have tried to live my life by an ethical code of conduct."

I will always remember Lee Iacocca's concept that optimism reigns, and it is more important how we succeed than how much we succeed.

It takes an optimist to go where no woman has gone before.

Sandra Day O'Connor was not well known outside judicial circles until that day in 1981 when she became the first woman to be confirmed to the U.S. Supreme Court. A moderate conservative, she rose through the ranks, first as an assistant attorney general, majority leader of the Arizona Senate (the first U.S. woman to hold such a post), and a Superior Court judge.

In answering my request for her viewpoint on success and optimism, Justice O'Connor sent me a transcript of an address she delivered to a college graduating class. Some of the points she was driving home to these new graduates are points we would do well to take.

> "The person who really impacts on this world is, as has always been the case, not an institution, not a committee, and not a person who just happens to have a title; rather, it is the truly qualitative individual. The qualitative individual *does* matter in this quantitative world of ours, now as ever."

Justice O'Connor went on to quote a passage from the Talmud that is also noteworthy:

> "In every age, there comes a time when leadership suddenly comes forth to meet the needs of the hour. And so there is no man who does not find his time, and there is no hour that does not have its leader."

In explaining this passage, Justice O'Connor said:

> "...Each of us, in our own individual lives and crises, will have a time to lead. Whether we will lead only a family, or a handful of friends,

and when and how we will lead, is up to us, our views, and our talents.

"...The very nature of humanity and society, regardless of its size or complexity, will always turn on the act of the individual and, therefore, on the quality of the individual."

You might scoff when you hear someone say, "One person can make a difference," but if an optimistic Supreme Court justice believes it can happen, I think we should start believing it, too.

You've heard it said that someone "needs no introduction," which is what is generally said before they give someone an introduction. Frank Sinatra needs no introduction but certainly deserves one.

I had the opportunity to meet and interview Frank Sinatra late in his life when he was doing a concert with the Dallas Symphony. We met at the hotel where he and his entourage were staying. They had blocked off the top two floors of the hotel for Mr. Sinatra. The police had cordoned off the streets in front of the hotel, and there were news helicopters circling the building.

I was in awe when I first met Frank Sinatra and quipped, "Mr. Sinatra, you've created quite a stir here in Dallas."

He seemed bewildered and asked one of his people, "Do you know what he's talking about?"

His longtime friend and bodyguard responded, "Yeah, boss. I know what he's talking about, but you don't."

It dawned on me that for over a half century, he had never been anywhere that wasn't in total turmoil because Frank Sinatra was the center of the hurricane his entire life.

Frank Sinatra was an Academy Award-winning actor and one of the top recording artists of all time, but his stardom went far beyond these accolades. Frank Sinatra was a force that impacted his industry and the world around him in a way that we may never see again. His optimistic legacy lives in his enduring songs such as "My Way," "New York, New York," and "High Hopes."

Here are a few thoughts Mr. Sinatra had drawing on his own experience and optimism.

"The best revenge is massive success.

"I would like to be remembered as a man who had a wonderful time living life, a man who had good friends, fine family—and I don't think I could ask for anything more than that, actually. People often remark that I'm pretty lucky. Luck is only important in so far as getting the chance to sell yourself at the right moment. After that, you've got to have talent and know how to use it. Throughout my career, if I have done anything, I have paid attention to every note and every word I sing—if I respect the song. If I cannot project this to a listener, I fail.

"I'm gonna live 'till I die."

When I concluded my interview with Frank Sinatra, he walked with me toward the elevator and left me with a phrase he was fond of saying instead of good-bye. "Hey kid, I hope you live to be 100 years old, and the last thing you hear is me singing you a song."

As a lifelong sports fan and National Champion Olympic Weightlifter myself, Bob Costas first came to my attention—as he did for people around the world—as the host of nine different Olympic Games. He has also been a prominent broadcast figure for the NFL, the NBA, and Major League Baseball as well as the US Open Golf Championship.

You can't observe that many top-level performers and champions in action without learning a lot about success and optimism. When I asked Bob Costas to draw on his expertise and provide some wisdom for me and you from his experience, he offered the following:

> "While we all choose our own paths in life, make our own mistakes, and achieve our own successes, one thing I believe is generally true—we do our best and end up happiest when the work we do reflects a genuine interest or passion. Our work is in some way an authentic extension of ourselves; better yet, if that work in some way touches or helps other people. One other thing I have learned along the way is that while high ideals and standards are important, and we can focus so disproportionately on that which is imperfect, we lose sight of much of what is good about ourselves and others. That's about as far

> as I will go since all of us are, to one extent or another, works in progress. And if we are at all self-aware, there are many times we find ourselves thinking, 'If I only knew or understood then, what I know and understand now.'"

The next time you're tuned in to a baseball, football, or basketball game or even the next Olympics and you hear the familiar voice of Bob Costas, remember what he knows now that he wishes he had known back then because you and I know it today.

Carol Channing has won three Tony awards including one for Lifetime Achievement, a Golden Globe Award, and has been nominated for an Academy Award.

Several years ago, I interviewed Carol Channing during her worldwide tour with *Hello, Dolly!* She has performed that role more than 25,000 times but still brings an energy and an excitement to it that is totally unique in the theatre. She's a perfect example of why I enjoy Broadway theatre both in New York and as presented by the touring companies. I am very proud that here at Narrative Television Network, through FM transmitters, we have opened the world of Broadway theatre to many blind and visually impaired people who otherwise might not have enjoyed this experience.

In all the years I've gone to the theatre, there was only one occasion when the audience gave a standing ovation in the middle of a performance. That was for Carol Channing in *Hello, Dolly!* When I asked her about this during our interview, she told me that it happened every night, and she optimistically thought audiences did that for everyone.

What does a performer like Carol Channing have to teach us besides maintaining unbridled enthusiasm? This is what she said to me:

> "Just keep working—keep working wherever you are.
>
> "I truly live for my work, and I'm fortunate to have a family that understands that. My husband understands it, my son understands it, and the dog understands it. Just live for it."

Believe me, when you have that sort of optimism about your work, the world will *stand up* and applaud.

Billy Joel has sold over 100 million albums, making him one of the bestselling recording artists of all time, and he has been inducted into the Rock and Roll Hall of Fame. The Broadway show entitled *Movin' Out* is based on Billy Joel's songs and his career.

As a musician, he creates the mood, but as a writer, he creates a message. You will discover some of his wit, wisdom, and optimism in his comments below.

> "I think music, in itself, is healing. It's an explosive expression of humanity. It's something we are all touched by. No matter what culture we're from, everyone loves music. I wish I were less of a thinking man and more of a fool not afraid of rejection.
>
> "Musicians want to be the loud voice for so many quiet hearts. If you make music for the human

needs you have within yourself, then you do it for all humans who need the same things. You enrich humanity with the profound expression of these feelings. As human beings, we need to know that we are not alone, that we are not crazy or completely out of our minds, that there are other people out there who feel as we do, live as we do, love as we do, who are like us.

"You're not the only one who has made mistakes, but they are the only things that you can truly call your own. I am no longer afraid of becoming lost, because the journey back always reveals something new, and that is ultimately good for the artist. Don't make music for some vast, unseen audience or market or ratings share or even for something as tangible as money. Though it's crucial to make a living, that shouldn't be your inspiration. Do it for yourself.

"The good ole days weren't always good, and tomorrow ain't as bad as it seems."

As someone who plays at playing the piano myself, I'm just good enough to respect someone like Billy Joel; however, when I think about his statement "I wish I were less of a thinking man and more of a fool not afraid of rejection," I realize that's the difference between playing at life and living it optimistically.

As I was pulling together this book, I studied a number of entertainment, business, political, and religious leaders.

I have to say that at the beginning I understood very little about the Dalai Lama. I still do not understand a great deal about his faith, but that's not what this book is about. It's about optimism, and that certainly shines through in all his thoughts, words, and deeds.

The Dalai Lama is a Tibetan religious leader. He won the Nobel Peace Prize in 1989 as a result of his appeals for nonviolent liberation of his homeland from Chinese rule. He faced exile for several decades, but he continues to write and speak about his faith and his search for peace.

When I contacted the Dalai Lama, I asked him the same question I ask everyone else I admire and want to emulate: What are your thoughts on success and optimism as you look back over your life and work? This is what he shared with me:

> "We have all been born on this earth as part of one great human family. Whatever the superficial differences that distinguish us, each of us is just a human being like everyone else. We all desire happiness and do not want suffering. What is more, each of us has an equal right to pursue these goals.

> "Because the very purpose of life is to be happy, it is important to discover what will bring about the greatest degree of happiness. Whether our experience is pleasant or miserable, it is either mental or physical. Generally, it is the mind that exerts the greatest influence on most of us;

therefore, we should devote our most serious efforts to bringing about mental peace. In my own limited experience, I have found that the greatest degree of inner tranquility comes from the development of love and compassion....

"The more we care for the happiness of others, the greater is our own sense of well-being. Cultivating a close, warm-hearted feeling for others automatically puts the mind at ease. This helps remove whatever fears or insecurities we may have and gives us the strength to cope with any obstacles we encounter. It is the ultimate source of happiness in life.

"I believe that at every level of society, from the family up to international relations, the key to a happier and more successful world is the nurturing of compassion. We do not need to become religious, nor do we need to believe in an ideology. All that is necessary is for each of us to develop our good human qualities."

These are optimistic words worth pondering regardless of our background, faith, or nationality. Optimism either works for everyone, or it doesn't work for anyone.

Jerry Glanville was a successful football player but best known as a coach for the NFL Houston Oilers and Atlanta Falcons. Later, he became a highly sought-after analyst for network television football broadcasts. He has the distinction of coining the phrase: NFL stands for "Not For Long."

Though he was criticizing a referee at the time, the phrase "Not For Long" has been adopted by many pro football players to express their thoughts about how short an athletic career can be and that one should optimistically enjoy every moment of every day.

When I asked Coach Glanville to share his own optimism thoughts of things he knows now he wishes he had known before, he drew on his coaching experience to condense his message into six brief points.

1. "Be positive about all opportunities.

2. "Never take credit.

3. "Discouragement cannot enter.

4. "Enjoy the moment.

5. "False praise cheapens real praise.

6. "Work harder than everyone who works with you."

Coach Glanville reminds us all that time is fleeting, and this life is "Not For Long"; therefore, we need to apply his six optimism principles and get the most out of every moment.

I believe all creative people are optimists. They accept what is but believe in and work toward what can be.

It might appear that Oleg Cassini peaked early. He was, after all, named the principle designer for First Lady

Jacqueline Kennedy in 1960. Decades later, however, he was still delighting customers with his unique designs.

Oleg Cassini had his first dress-designing success when he was 13 and living in Italy. He moved to the U.S. in 1936 but had trouble catching on in New York, so he moved to Hollywood and began designing costumes for the movie studios. He returned to New York in 1950, became a hit, and never looked back.

Many of the well-known people I've talked with have told me that their "secret" of optimism and success is something they read or heard elsewhere. Oleg Cassini was no exception. He found inspiration in the Rudyard Kipling poem "If" and said he especially focused on the line I've highlighted.

For several years, I have given Kipling's famous poem to young people and offered them a cash reward to read the poem and write a report about what it means to them. As a fan of poetry and sometime-poet myself, I think it may be among the best examples of the genre. Let me share with you part of this great poem.

IF

If you can keep your head when all about you
Are losing theirs and blaming it on you,
If you can trust yourself when all men doubt you,
But make allowance for their doubting, too;
If you can wait and not be tired by waiting,
Or being lied about, don't deal in lies,

Or being hated, don't give way to hating,
And yet don't look too good, nor talk too wise:

If you can dream—and not make
dreams your master;
If you can think—and not make thoughts your aim;
If you can meet with Triumph and Disaster
And treat those two imposters just the same….

If you can talk with crowds and keep your virtue,
Or walk with Kings—nor lose the common touch,
If neither foes nor loving friends can hurt you,
If all men count with you, but none too much;
If you can fill the unforgiving minute
With sixty seconds' worth of distance run,
Yours is the Earth and everything that's in it,
And—which is more—you'll be a Man, my son!

Oleg Cassini passed away a few years ago. He is gone but will never be forgotten as long as people look at photos and video from the Camelot era of the Kennedy administration or enjoy great films from the Golden Age of the movie industry.

In the U.S., you don't get much more successful than being named Secretary of State. And you don't get chosen for that post unless you have outstanding credentials and experience.

Alexander Haig more than met the requirements of the job. He was, after all, a graduate of the U.S. Military

Academy, the Naval War College, and the Army War College. He became a general in 1973, was chief of staff at the White House, and served as commander-in-chief of the U.S. European Command. He was definitely someone you want to talk to when you are writing a book on optimism.

In responding to my request for his comments, this is what he said:

> "Whatever you do, make a difference.

> "Practice rather than preach. Be a realist but only to change the world guided by your principles. There is justice though often well-disguised. Make of your life an affirmation, defined by your ideals, not the negation of others. Dare to the level of your capability, then go beyond to a higher level.

> "If you would be fit to command men, obey God."

I might add, if you can't be a leader, be the best follower you can possibly be. When you do your best, you are an optimist.

I was born and raised in Tulsa, Oklahoma, where I make my home to this day. The most famous Tulsan of all time may well have been Paul Harvey. He began working on the air at a local radio station when he was still in high school. Ironically, I do a weekly radio program that is carried on that same station today. Paul Harvey's talent, tenacity, and optimism soon put him on the national and the world stage.

For several generations of people, Paul Harvey *News and Comment* was a daily fixture. People gathered around radios each morning and midday to hear the news delivered to them as if Paul Harvey were their neighbor talking across the back fence. His "rest of the story" broadcasts let listeners look behind the façade of the people, places, and events they thought they knew to learn the deeper truths beyond.

I met Paul Harvey when he called my office after reading one of my books. When my phone buzzed and they told me that Paul Harvey was calling, I thought, *It's a common name*, but I asked, "Is it *the* Paul Harvey?"

The immediate response was, "I don't think anyone else can talk like that."

Paul Harvey endorsed several of my books and became a mentor and friend. He was one of the best speakers I ever heard. Whether he was speaking from the stage or his radio microphone, Mr. Harvey made everyone feel as if he were speaking directly to them.

He never took his mission or his message for granted. Every time he broadcast the news, he did so standing at a podium wearing a suit and tie. He told me, "Whether I'm going to church, out on the town with my beloved bride Angel, or talking to my friends on the radio, I believe in dressing like it matters…because it does."

Mr. Harvey wrote much of the news copy he read to us on the radio for years. He had the unique talent of capturing complex thoughts and emotions in a brief phrase. Here's Mr. Harvey's optimism in headline form.

> "In times like these, it helps to recall that there have always been times like these.

> "Like what you do. If you don't like it, do something else.

> "When your outgo exceeds your income, the upshot may be your downfall.

> "Every pessimist who ever lived has been buried in an unmarked grave. Tomorrow has always been better than today, and it always will be.

> "I've never seen a monument erected to a pessimist.

> "Retiring is just practicing up to be dead. That doesn't take any practice."

Paul Harvey became famous for his signature signoff at the end of each broadcast. He would finish a news story and then announce, "Paul Harvey," followed by a long pause and then end his broadcast with the simple optimistic admonition, "Good day."

He told me as a rookie broadcaster, his manager's only advice before his first-ever live newscast was to simply read the script exactly and finish precisely at the top of the hour. Apparently, Mr. Harvey had several seconds left over at the end of that inaugural broadcast and just remained silent 'til the top of the hour, leaving what he liked to call his "pregnant pause."

The last time I ever spoke to him on the phone, he left me with the words he left to the world throughout his life. "Good day!"

Tom Osborne has served three terms in the United States House of Representatives, but he will always be remembered as the head coach of the Nebraska Cornhuskers where he led the team for over 25 years, winning three national championships and being inducted into the College Football Hall of Fame.

Growing up in Oklahoma and following the beloved Oklahoma Sooners, I remember Tom Osborne as the coach who led the dreaded Nebraska team into all the fierce rivalry games with Oklahoma. All of the games were classics, but one of the Oklahoma/Nebraska games has actually become known by the experts as "the game of the century."

Being a great coach, Tom Osborne draws on the wisdom of others and brings his own optimism to that wisdom.

> "The advice I often pass on to young people does not originate from me. Rather, it is a quote from Warren Buffett who often tells young people to 'invest in yourself.' This type of investment has to do with acquiring as much education as possible, surrounding oneself with people of wisdom and sound character, and engaging in activities which produce physical, intellectual, and spiritual growth."

Nebraska is a relatively small state with respect to population, but any state that has optimistic residents such as Warren Buffett and Tom Osborne doesn't have to take a backseat to anyone.

T. Boone Pickens is a billionaire and an optimist. It's important to remember that his optimism became a part of his life before his money did. He has over a half century of experience in business, but he remains on the cutting edge of technology and global influence. One need look no further than the news to see that T. Boone Pickens is called upon for his experience relating to the past and his optimism relating to the future.

He wanted me to share this with you:

> "More than eight decades on this earth has taught me a thing or two. Here are a few that I hope might be meaningful, no matter what the individual circumstances:
>
> *"America remains the greatest country in the world.* There's more opportunity for success today than ever.
>
> *"Don't think competition is bad, but play by the rules.* I love to compete and win. I don't want the other guy to do badly; I just want to do a little better than he does.
>
> *"Learn to analyze well.* Assess the risks and the prospective awards, and keep it simple. Be willing to make decisions. That's the most

important quality in a good leader: Avoid the 'Ready-aim-aim-aim' syndrome. You have to be willing to fire.

"*Learn from mistakes.* That's not just a cliché. Remember the doors that smashed your fingers the first time, and be more careful the next trip through.

"*Embrace change.* Although older people are generally threatened by change, young people love me because I embrace change rather than running from it."

Great advice comes from people who have been to the mountaintop, and even greater advice comes from those who are using their perspective from the summit to optimistically look toward the next mountain.

Dr. Oz is an eminent physician widely respected by his colleagues, but he has become the doctor to the masses due to his numerous television appearances. As usual, his advice is optimistic, balanced, and practical. His optimistic outlook brings us a prescription for living a healthy, happy, and successful life.

"My advice for those just beginning their journey to success would be to have the goal of a healthy living philosophy—which should be to achieve and maintain physical and mental wellness. This can be achieved with a healthy diet, exercise, a strong social life, and the occasional indulgence. Diet and exercise keeps the body healthy and can prevent disabling diseases like heart disease and diabetes. Additionally, exercise boosts endorphins, a hormone in the body that promotes happiness and can decrease depression. Exercising 30 minutes per day for 5 days a week should be enough to feel the benefits. Another thing that is really important is having a strong social network with supporting family and friends. Feeling loved and loving others can promote a sense of belonging, increase self-worth, and feelings of security. All of these support wellness, and when your mind and body are healthy, you can achieve anything!"

Here in the 21st century, we deal with medical breakthroughs and miracles that would have seemed like science fiction just a few years ago, but before we look to space-age medicine, it's good to take Dr. Oz's down-to-earth optimistic advice on living well.

Barbra Streisand is the bestselling American female recording artist of all time. Her honors include an Emmy, an Oscar, and more gold records than any other recording artist. She has mastered stage, screen, and the music industry for five decades.

Few people have seen the world from the perch Barbra Streisand enjoys, and this gives her tremendous wisdom and optimism.

"There is nothing more important in life than love.

"Doubt can motivate you, so don't be afraid of it. Confidence and doubt are at the two ends of the scale, and you need both. They balance each other out. I've been called many names like perfectionist, difficult, and obsessive. I think it takes obsession, takes searching for the details for any artist to be good. You have to discover you, what you do, and trust it. There's always a part of you that remains a child, no matter how mature you get, how sophisticated, or how weary.

"I arrived in Hollywood without having my nose fixed, my teeth capped, or my name changed. That is very gratifying to me."

Barbra Streisand might be challenging to work with, but the final results are always worth the effort.

You've met a number of optimists in this chapter, but if I were forced to pick only one individual as the emperor of optimism, it would be the late, great Zig Ziglar. Zig was an encouragement to me as a fellow speaker, author, and businessperson, but even more, he was a friend.

Zig had a faith, enthusiasm, and optimism that impacted everyone around him. His words live on and will change lives for generations to come.

"Your attitude, not your aptitude, will determine your altitude.

"People often say that motivation doesn't last. Well, neither does bathing—that's why we recommend it daily.

"The foundation stones for a balanced success are honesty, character, integrity, faith, love, and loyalty.

"You can make positive deposits in your own economy every day by reading and listening to powerful, positive, life-changing content and by associating with encouraging and hope-building people.

"Be grateful for what you have and stop complaining. It bores everybody else, does you no good, and doesn't solve any problems.

"When you encourage others, you—in the process—are encouraged because you're making a commitment and difference in that person's life. Encouragement really does make a difference.

"You can have everything in life you want if you will just help other people get what they want.

"Time can be an ally or an enemy. What it becomes depends entirely upon you, your goals, and your determination to use every available minute."

Zig Ziglar's books, videos, and speeches were among the most impactful in the profession because they weren't just words, thoughts, or ideas to Zig. They were his life.

Any time you get discouraged and wonder if optimists are real people, you can revisit this chapter and meet some real optimists again.

CHAPTER SIX

THE PESSIMISM
PRESCRIPTION

*"The more man meditates upon
good thoughts, the better will be his
world and the world at large."*
—CONFUCIUS

Now that you have met some optimists and you understand that optimism is our natural state, all we need to do is stamp out pessimism, and that which remains will be genuine optimism.

There are many in the world today who have been pessimistic for so long that they doubt whether things can ever change. Optimism is, indeed, our natural state, and those pessimistic individuals have allowed negative influences to change their worldview.

Martin Seligman, considered one of the pillars of modern psychology, spent the early years of his practice chronicling the detrimental impact of depression, stress, and anxiety. His research revealed that being an optimist, in essence, immunized or protected a person from the influence of depression.

As he began to understand how important optimism was to mental health, he set out to determine whether or not pessimism could be eliminated and optimism could replace it as a patient's permanent worldview. Dr. Seligman committed the latter part of his career to studies that proved pessimism can be replaced by optimism.

Following this theory, a curriculum was developed in what has become known as the Penn Resiliency Program. It was thought that—because school-aged students were still developing—they might be in a sense vaccinated against pessimism resulting in an optimistic future.

School faculty and staff were trained to administer pre- and post-tests and teach a 12-week course that taught students how to control their thoughts and observe circumstances in a more positive light. At the end of the 12 weeks, the same students were retested, and by a statistically significant number, pessimistic students were thinking optimistically. In order to further verify these results, these same students were tested every six months over the ensuing three years. The optimistic results held true, and this study was repeated in several middle school and high school settings.

The evidence seems clear that pessimism can change, and we can return to our natural state of optimism.

Scientists since the beginning of the field of psychology have argued whether children develop as a result of nature or nurture. The debate rages on today as to whether we are most influenced in our formative years by our genetics or by environmental factors around us.

In any event, whether children are influenced by nature or nurture, the reality remains that adults are influenced by their choices. As we explored earlier, I fully understand that bad things happen to good people, and some individuals suffered through pessimistic and even horrific childhoods, but regardless of our past, you and I can change our lives by changing our minds this very moment.

Your pessimism may have been caused by influences in your childhood, but as an adult you now own your pessimism and can trade it in for optimism whenever you want. Most people don't realize they have this choice or option. They assume that their attitudes, outlooks, and worldviews are a permanent and static part of their environment. Just as you can change your faith, political views, clothing styles, or food preferences, you can change the lens through which you see the world and build your future.

It's important to understand that optimism and pessimism are not black and white factors. It's not like turning on the light, and a dark room suddenly becomes illuminated. There are various shades and degrees of both optimism and pessimism, so whether you find yourself as a deep, dark pessimist or a moderate optimist who would like to take full advantage of the success benefits that optimism offers, it's within your control, and it all begins with a simple choice.

I tell my audiences at arena events and corporate conventions, "You change your life when you change your mind, you are one quality decision away from anything you want, and you have the right to choose."

People often are skeptical and ask, "Is it really that simple?" The answer is that it is, indeed, very simple, but it is never easy. Changing a pessimistic attitude to an optimistic attitude involves the simple decision to do so followed by consistent and ongoing diligence to control our thoughts and the influences around us.

Optimism is a state of mind not to be confused with motivation, which is an emotion. Pessimists can be motivated after an enlightening speech, uplifting book, or positive movie, but in a few minutes or hours they will revert back to their worldview as a pessimist. Conversely, optimists can suffer loss or tragedy and temporarily have an emotion of grief or sadness but will emerge with their optimistic worldview intact and begin to look for the good in the midst of a bad situation.

The instant you decide to become an optimist, it is like striking a spark that has energy and potential, but unless you feed that spark with fuel and keep detrimental elements away from it, it will quickly be extinguished, and you will return to the dark world of pessimism.

I will assume by virtue of the fact you are still reading these words that you have made such a decision and currently have at least a spark of optimism that we can fan into a flame or even a raging inferno of optimistic energy and power that can fuel your life and your dreams.

Among the most powerful and practical recent discoveries in the field of behavioral science is the fact that we become like the five people with whom we spend the most time. Our interests, speech patterns, career development, and income will begin to approximate the average of these five influencers we have around us. What's more important is that our worldview of optimism or pessimism will be fed and influenced by these five individuals.

In my office at home, I have a long, thin poster that is approximately a foot wide and five feet long. It was given to me by a dear friend and colleague. At the top of the poster, it has a bold heading proclaiming "Success is..." Down the length of the poster are listed the many factors in the world that make up and define success. Number one on the list is "Marry the right person."

No matter your worldview, external thoughts, or attitudes, you will be most influenced by the person you have chosen to spend your life with. I highly recommend you connect with your spouse or significant other and include them on this journey into the world of optimism.

Once you have identified your five influencers around you, you may need to make some changes. If you made a decision to stop smoking, begin exercising, or improve your diet and you don't at least communicate with the five closest people around you, you will find it very difficult to change these habits. In a much deeper, more significant way, optimism and pessimism are influenced and reinforced by your influential five people.

You may discover that one of your closest friends or even a family member is a devout pessimist and not willing to change. This doesn't mean you have to eliminate them from your life, but it may require you to limit your time with them and control your environment when you are exposed to their pessimism.

There are times when we are more vulnerable to pessimism than other times. For me as I dictate these words, I'm keenly aware that the writing process represents one of my most vulnerable times. There are certain friends, associates, and family members who won't hear from me while I am writing a book, creating a movie, or preparing for a speech. At these times, I substitute one-way communication for dialogue.

When I am in my creative phase, the people closest to me who have chosen a life of pessimism are likely to get an email or a greeting card as opposed to a phone call or lunch invitation. Your optimism is the most important asset you have, and you've got to protect it, particularly when it is only a tiny spark. When you become a fully-engaged and committed lifelong optimist, you can deal with much more pessimistic influence, but while you're in the formative stages of your optimism development, you must guard your environment.

For over 20 years, I have been a part of an accountability group with several powerful individuals I met in college. Every other Sunday night, we have an in-depth conference call and discuss one another's goals, commitments, and priorities. These individuals can say anything to me, and I, in turn, can say anything to them. I totally trust their judgment and their motives. This is a completely safe zone for my optimism.

In each of my endeavors, I surround myself with what I call a dream team. It is much like the mastermind concept introduced by Napoleon Hill in his book *Think and Grow Rich*. My dream teams are made up of people who have been where I want to go and who are committed to me and my success.

When I prepared to launch my core business, the Narrative Television Network, which you will learn a little bit about in an upcoming chapter, I tried to think of the biggest innovators and successful role models in the TV industry. The first name that came to my mind was Ted Turner. His success in cable television and the media in general was unparalleled, so I wrote him a brief letter sharing my hopes and goals, and I am pleased to say he was willing to help then as he does now.

When I ventured into the financial realm with my writing, speaking, and movies, I once again considered what individual in that arena might be the best person to anchor my dream team. The first individual who came to mind was Steve Forbes. Through his *Forbes* magazine and other publications, he is arguably the most powerful person in the fields of money, wealth, and success. When I shared my goals and objectives with Mr. Forbes, he agreed to give me his input, and that was the beginning of what now is one of my great friendships and mentor relationships.

When we started being contacted by movie studios that were interested in turning my books into movies, I tried to think of the individuals I admire and respect most in that industry. I am pleased that I have been able to collaborate with and learn from individuals such as James Garner, Peter Fonda, Raquel Welch, and Academy Award-winner Louis Gossett, Jr. The influence of your dream team will not only create a quantum leap in your learning and your contacts but will help to secure your optimism as you move forward toward your goal.

Once you have considered the people with whom you work and live with respect to optimism, it is important that you control the thoughts and images that bombard us all via books, magazines, television, movies, and online sources.

More than any other generation that came before us, we are under constant attack from outside influences. The Internet alone can bring you the very best or the very worst of what the world has to offer. Your computer or smartphone makes a great slave but a horrible master. If you are to control your worldview, you must take control of your environment.

I am in the television business, and for years in my speeches to colleagues and in articles I have written, I have maintained that the television industry lies. TV executives have maintained for years that although they constantly show a steady stream of violence, deceit, and demeaning messages, it really doesn't affect the audience because they know it's not real. On the other hand, these same individuals will tell advertisers that if they will just buy a 30-second commercial, it will change the products and services you buy as well as what you think and even who you will vote for. We all have access to on-demand or recorded TV programming, so there's no excuse for letting anything into your home that doesn't feed or nurture your optimism.

I remember a powerful image shared by the great author and speaker Earl Nightingale in his influential success course *Lead the Field*. Mr. Nightingale described seeing one of the world's largest earthmoving machines. It was several stories high with a shovel the size of an average house. This outsized machine was used to mine coal and could literally move mountains.

Mr. Nightingale told about standing on a distant hilltop as he watched this immense mechanical marvel reforming the landscape. Through binoculars, he could see a tiny speck seated high atop the machine, which was the driver who controlled all the power and energy by simply twisting a few dials and levers.

Earl Nightingale used that example more than 50 years ago to explain the power of our mind. I believe if Earl were still alive today and was using the same example, the driver who controlled the power and energy of the enormous earthmoving machine would be wearing a headset or earbuds as he listened to music or a message that controlled his thoughts that, in turn, controlled his actions that, in turn, controlled the machine that, in turn, could change the world around it.

Movies have become one of the most iconic worldwide influencers. Phrases such as "What we've got here is a failure to communicate," "Here's looking at you kid," and "Toto, I don't think we're in Kansas anymore," were uttered briefly in movie theaters over a half century ago and now are permanent fixtures in the world's vernacular. Movies create a constant reality that in some ways is more influential than the real world around us.

My late, great friend and colleague Zig Ziglar defined fear as F.E.A.R. or False Evidence Appearing Real. If we go to a frightening, brutal horror movie, we may be sitting next to our friends or family munching popcorn, but the images on the screen begin to work upon our mind and attitude. Before we realize it, the movie will begin to make physiological changes in our body. Our heart rate and respiration will increase, blood pressure will elevate, and we will break out in a cold sweat. If a piece of film can make physical, measurable changes in us, how much more can those images alter our attitudes and world view both immediately and long into the future.

It's impossible to calculate the impact of an optimistic or pessimistic word, phrase, or image years into the future. I remember my grandmother constantly encouraging me by saying, "Let me tell you about my grandson." Then she would list all my Little League accomplishments, scouting badges, and the positive aspects of my report card. It seemed insignificant to me at the time, but that brief phrase can instantly propel me back to that time and place in my grandmother's home hearing those words.

After the success of my first few books, I was asked to give a motivational speech at a prison. After the speech, the warden asked me and one of the other speakers—a professional baseball player—if we would go downstairs and visit some of the inmates on death row who had not been permitted to leave their cells to attend the speeches in the auditorium.

I will never forget walking down the aisle between those tiny cells and greeting each of the inmates.

One prisoner asked the baseball player beside me, "When did you first know you would end up in the Big Leagues?"

The ball player responded, "From my earliest memories, my dad told me I could make it, and I would end up where I am."

The death row prisoner sighed and responded through the iron bars, "Yeah. My dad told me I would end up here, too."

We must control the negative assaults on our optimism, and then we have to replace the pessimistic input with constant messages, images, and positive input that builds our optimistic future.

CHAPTER SEVEN

FUELING OUR OPTIMISM

*"I believe any success in life is
made by going into an area with
a blind, furious optimism."*
—SYLVESTER STALLONE

All of us are born with a proverbial gold medal hanging around our neck. Our medal has an inscription on it that reads: *I am lovable, capable, and able to do anything I want to do.*

As an infant, this is all we know and all we need to know, and then the world around us rushes in, and other people begin writing on our medal covering up the original inscription. They write things like: *You are stupid*; *You are strange*; and *You're never going to accomplish anything.* These new messages written on the gold medal hanging around our neck begin to pull us down and become a self-fulfilling prophecy.

As we learned in the previous chapter, we can avoid, eliminate, or eradicate negative messages. We can wipe those pessimistic words off our medal leaving it with a shiny blank surface, but it won't stay blank for long. The universe abhors a void. Any void we leave behind will be immediately filled with the most readily available material possible. So, if we get rid of bad messages and fail to replace those messages with positive, optimistic messages, the negative input will return to us immediately.

If you have ever tried meditation, you know that the first step and the hardest step is to clear your mind. Your mind naturally wants to be filled with input and information. People who habitually meditate can clear their minds for brief periods each day, but it's impossible to make your mind a blank slate for very long.

I have the ability to think about anything and everything, but I can't constantly think about nothing, so as we clear pessimism from our minds we must replace it with optimism; and because our modern world is filled with much more pessimism than optimism, this process represents a worthy challenge.

Music offers great opportunities for optimism. Music reaches our brain in a different way than other data or information. Many of us learned the alphabet through singing it to the melody of "Twinkle, Twinkle Little Star." To this day, if I'm pressed to put several random things in alphabetical order, I find myself humming that melody. You probably don't remember what you had for dinner three nights ago, but if I were to play some songs that were popular during your senior year of high school, you would invariably discover that you remember lyrics to songs you haven't heard in years or even decades.

Music can be the soundtrack of your life and success. As a teenager, my parents took me to New York City, and we got to visit Carnegie Hall. There wasn't a concert going on, but a quartet was practicing, and we were able to stand in the back of the hall for a few moments. I heard the most empowering and uplifting piece of music I had ever experienced. Years later, I discovered that it was called the "Canon in D" and was written by a German church organist named Pachelbel. For almost 300 years, this one piece of music has ranked high among successful individuals who use music as a foundation stone for their optimism. If you don't like classical music, there are many other choices.

As a former athlete, I spent much of my time as a teenager and young adult in locker rooms. If you were to visit any professional or college team's locker room before a big game, you would find many of the players listening to music on a headset or using earbuds. They are all hoping to be motivated and use the music as a way to focus on their performance; but although they have the same goals, they utilize vastly different input. Some team members may be listening to rap while others listen to rock, and some may be listening to country music or even white noise.

There is a clear delineation between optimistic and pessimistic music, and since it goes directly into your mind and remains an indelible part of your thinking, it's important to make the right selections. If you have not taken a moment to listen to the lyrics of some of the most popular tunes played today, you would be shocked at many of the violent and destructive messages. You may think you're not listening to the lyrics, so you're just enjoying the melody, but your mind is organizing those tunes with those words. Remember, "Twinkle, Twinkle Little Star" is your memory key for the alphabet. If you're not selective about the music you're listening to, it will be your memory key to hatred and violence as opposed to love, success, and possibilities.

As we discovered in a previous chapter, reading is the input most successful people utilize to bring themselves pure, positive, and powerful messages. Whenever you have the privilege of meeting someone who is successful or has achieved something you desire in your own life, be sure to ask them what books they read when they were getting started and what they are reading today.

There are countless suggested reading lists available on the Internet showing what peak performers have read. I would suggest that you spend a set amount of time reading each day. I'm not talking about reading the latest popular thriller for entertainment. I'm talking about reading as an antidote to pessimism and as your fuel for optimism. There's certainly nothing wrong with reading for entertainment, and you may well find optimistic books to be the most entertaining ones you ever read.

Movies create the most vivid images of any media available to us. If you think of your favorite movie, you will likely see, hear, and feel it unfolding in your mind. You can call up these positive, optimistic movie images whenever you want them. Unfortunately, if you're not careful, pessimistic movie images will invade your consciousness at the least opportune moment.

I regularly watch movies such as *Chariots of Fire*, *Rudy*, or the *Rocky* film series as I find them motivational and optimistic. You can create your own movie playlist. If you're looking for a few suggestions, at the risk of being self-serving, my book entitled *The Lamp* and the movie based on it starring Academy Award-winner Louis Gossett, Jr. can bring you powerful, positive, and optimistic images every time you watch it.

My novel *The Ultimate Gift* and the sequels, which we turned into the movie trilogy *The Ultimate Gift*, *The*

Ultimate Life, and *The Ultimate Legacy*, are positive favorites of many individuals and families around the world. These movies are also used in schools and corporate settings where an uplifting success message that is also engaging and entertaining is called for.

Below are the key elements of *The Ultimate Gift* and a power statement for each. I know many people who display these powerful words in their home or office so they can be constantly reminded of the optimistic messages.

In the Beginning.
A journey may be long or short,
but it must start at the very spot one finds oneself.

A Voice from the Past.
In the end,
a person is only known
by the impact they have on others.

The Gift of Work.
He who loves his work never labors.

The Gift of Money.
Money is nothing more than a tool.
It can be a force for good, a force for evil,
or simply be idle.

The Gift of Friends.
It is a wealthy person, indeed,

who calculates riches not in gold
but in friends.

The Gift of Learning.
Education is a lifelong journey
whose destination expands as you travel.

The Gift of Problems.
Problems may only be avoided by
exercising good judgment.
Good judgment may only be gained
by experiencing life's problems.

The Gift of Family.
Some people are born into wonderful families.
Others have to find or create them.
Being a member of a family is a priceless membership
that we pay nothing for but love.

The Gift of Dreams.
Faith is all that dreamers need
to see into the future.

The Gift of Laughter
Laughter is good medicine for the soul.
Our world is desperately in need
of more such medicine.

The Gift of Giving.
The only way you can truly get
more out of life for yourself
is to give part of yourself away.

The Gift of Gratitude.
In those times we yearn to have more in our lives,
we should dwell on the things we already have.
In doing so, we will often find that our lives
are already full to overflowing.

The Gift of a Day.
Life at its essence boils down to one day at a time.
Today is the day!

The Gift of Love.
Love is a treasure for which we can never pay.
The only way we keep it is to give it away.

The Ultimate Gift.
In the end, life lived to its fullest
is its own Ultimate Gift.

Poetry can evoke some of the most vivid images of optimism that we can find anywhere. In Chapter 5, Oleg Cassini presented us with what I feel to be one of the most optimistic, success-affirming poems of all time, Rudyard Kipling's "If."

As a blind person myself, all my 40 books, the movie screenplays based on my novels, and 20 years' worth of weekly syndicated columns including the words you are reading this moment have been dictated to my very talented colleague Dorothy Thompson. Dorothy not only types everything I dictate, but she is the most talented editor and grammarian I have ever encountered.

Several years ago, we were working on one of my books when a phone call informed Dorothy that her elderly mother was in critical condition. She was advised that if she wanted to see her mother again, she should come immediately. Dorothy made the trip to another state in time to spend some quality hours with her mother.

Dorothy's mother told Dorothy and her sister of a box on the top shelf of her closet that they should go through after she passed. After their mother's funeral, Dorothy and her sister opened the box and discovered a lifetime of poetry that had been written throughout her mother's life. When Dorothy read me a few of her mother's poems, I instantly knew they were not only meaningful to Dorothy because they had been penned by her mother, but they would be meaningful to a whole generation of readers.

I wrote a book entitled *Discovering Joye,* which featured the poetry of Dorothy's mother, Joye Kanelakos. Several of her poems are powerful instruments to bring you instant optimism whenever you need a boost.

This poem should be the optimist's anthem of how to start your day.

I awoke this morning
With a prayer of gratefulness;

A prayer of hopefulness
And joy.
To a God of love—
I asked for Love—
A house filled with it.
I seek and expect a home
Bursting its seams and lifting the roof with Love,
Driving out everything else
And making a place for angels to enter
And sing of the promise:
"Where love is, there I am also."

If you're looking for a mantra for an optimistic life, this poem of Joye's is for you.

How are You?
I am as healthy as I believe myself to be.
I am as wealthy as I believe.
I am only as blessed as I consider myself blessed.
I am as happy as I will allow myself to become.
My life is as productive as I, myself, will permit.

In this poem, Joye artistically echoes Coach Wooden's admonition, "Things turn out best for those who make the best of the way things turn out." Read it and imagine the possibilities.

Hidden paths,
obscured by fears,
grown over by habits of worry

and negativity from doubt,
begin to appear and invite us.
These paths are our great opportunities.
Our destinies.
Our inheritance waiting for us.
This is our "good luck" we have sought forever.

When I wrote *Discovering Joye*, I couldn't help but include a couple of my own offerings. In my ethereal novel, *The Keeper of the Flame*, I wrote about an obscure musician who met an unknown poet long before they both came to world prominence and artistic acclaim. In the story, the musician offers the poet the opportunity to experience one of his new compositions. The poet, in gratitude, offers the musician these thoughts.

CORNERSTONES

by Jim Stovall

If I am to dream, let me dream magnificently.
Let me dream grand and lofty thoughts and ideals
That are worthy of me and my best efforts.

If I am to strive, let me strive mightily.
Let me spend myself and my very being
In a quest for that magnificent dream.

And, if I am to stumble, let me stumble but persevere.
Let me learn, grow, and expand myself

to join the battle renewed—
Another day and another day and another day.

If I am to win, as I must, let me do so
with honor, humility, and gratitude
For those people and things that
have made winning possible
And so very sweet.

For each of us has been given life
as an empty plot of ground
With four cornerstones.
These four cornerstones are the ability to dream,
The ability to strive,
The ability to stumble but persevere,
And the ability to win.

The common man sees his plot
of ground as little more
Than a place to sit and ponder the
things that will never be.
But the uncommon man sees his
plot of ground as a castle,
A cathedral,
A place of learning and healing.

For the uncommon man understands
that in these four cornerstones
The Almighty has given us
anything—and everything.

Poetry gives us immediate access to optimistic imagery. I end all my speeches with this poem I wrote as a call to action for my audience.

HOLD ON TO YOUR DREAMS

by Jim Stovall

Hold on to your dreams and stand tall,
Even when those around you
would force you to crawl.
Hold on to your dreams as a race you must run
Even when reality whispers, "You'll never be done."
Hold on to your dreams and wait
for the miracles to come,
Because on that miraculous day,
Your dreams and your reality will merge into one.

We all have a master scrapbook within our minds. This scrapbook features selected images from our past. Pessimists retain memories of their failures, shortcomings, disappointments, and times they have been insulted or abused. Optimists collect memories of their victories, milestones, celebrations, and triumphs. In my own scrapbook, when needed I can call up the images, emotions, and feelings of when I received a gold medal as the national champion Olympic weightlifter, when I received an Emmy award for our work at the Narrative Television Network, when I received an honorary Doctorate from the university I had dropped out of as a visually impaired person but returned to get my degree as a blind person, or the opening of the Stovall Center on that same university campus.

Your optimistic scrapbook can overcome all manner of challenges. We all hear those two eternal voices. One repeats *You are lovable, capable, and able to do anything you choose to do,* and the other proclaims *You are ugly, stupid, and will continue to fail in the future.* Choosing which voice we will listen to is a function of optimism or pessimism. We can control this through revisiting great memories, powerful moments, and monumental achievements.

Whenever I am tempted to feel sorry for myself, I remember my encounter with Christopher Reeve. We were hired to be the opening and closing keynote speakers for *The Million Dollar Roundtable,* which is among the most prestigious platform speaking opportunities each year.

As a blind person myself, memorizing a new arena or convention-center stage for each event and not having access to notes, teleprompters, or any other visual input can be somewhat daunting. But after I worked with Christopher Reeve, I pledged to never feel sorry for myself again.

He had come to world prominence bringing Superman back to life on the silver screen. Then after a horrible riding accident, he found himself living life in a wheelchair unable to move or even breathe on his own. When I learned of all the preparations and advance work he and his team had to do before each appearance, I recognized then—as I do now—how lucky I am. You may have watched Superman on the big screen in a theatre, but you never fully experienced Superman unless you got to see Christopher Reeve at a live event.

Sometimes, in the midst of our trials and tribulations, if we are going to stay optimistic, we need to be able to laugh at ourselves. One of the first times I went out to make a speech after losing my sight is just such an incident.

My colleague Kathy and I had been building the Narrative Television Network, and we had sought counsel from a public relations firm on how to promote our work. They told me that as the president of this new network and as the on-air host of the talk show, it was customary for me to go out and meet each of the station managers who carried our programming.

We had over 1,000 affiliates at that time, and I was just getting out of my 9- by 12-foot room. I could navigate the office each day, but the thought of being on the road to visit hundreds and hundreds of television stations seemed impossible. So, I informed our PR firm that they would have to come up with another plan.

A few weeks later, they presented a unique alternative. They said, "Instead of you going around to meet all of our station managers, we're going to book you into convention centers, arenas, and corporate events as a motivational speaker; and then we'll invite in all of our station managers on a regional basis to be our guests."

They went on to explain, "That way, we can kill two birds with one stone."

I never was totally clear on why we wanted to kill birds with stones, but it seemed very important to our PR firm at the time.

That is when I asked the question that gets us all in trouble here in the 21st century. I asked, "When would I have to start?"

Although I was terrified at the thought of walking into a strange arena to make a speech, when they told me that events are scheduled at least six months in advance—and I wouldn't have to do anything until sometime next year—I readily agreed to their plan. My schedule is, I'm sure, much like yours is in that there are days when I don't know what I'm doing an hour in the future. So, when they asked me to make a commitment six months in advance, I readily agreed. Unfortunately, I will agree to anything that is that far in the future.

I promptly forgot about our public relations firm and the speeches I had agreed to make, and went about my daily business. What seemed like a few days, or certainly no more than a few weeks later, they came back down the hall to my office and said, "Jim, it's time to go."

I was a bit bewildered and asked, "Go where?"

They explained that it was time to go make one of the speeches that I had committed to making. I protested, saying, "You guys promised me it would be at least six months before I had to go make a speech."

They tried to assure me by saying, "Trust us. It has been a full six months."

You see, they always lie to the blind guy, and they think they get away with it—and in reality they do. I just like to let them know I know they get away with it.

I resigned myself to the task at hand and asked, "Who am I making the speech for?"

They informed me that I would be traveling to Anaheim, California, where I would be the motivational speaker for a group of 14,000 state government workers. At this point, I hasten to add, if you have ever been a state government worker, know any state government workers, or actually even discovered anyone doing any work for the state government, I will ask you to please excuse my next statement. But I thought being the motivational speaker for state government workers was something akin to raising the dead.

A bit of a daunting task, to say the least.

All the arrangements were made, and I found myself standing backstage getting ready to go out and give a speech. Kathy had accompanied me on the trip and was standing backstage with me as I was mentally going through the dimensions of the stage.

As I was trying to remember if it was 12 steps or 13 to the front of the platform, and other critical little tidbits of information, I began to sense someone standing next to me. As a blind person, you become very aware of things around you, and standing backstage, I could just sense someone standing very close to me, even though they weren't making any noise.

If you and I have an opportunity to meet at some point in the future, I will warn you now—you have got to make noise. If you don't make noise, you and I are going to have some real problems.

As I was trying to get over my terror, thinking about the upcoming speech, I couldn't get over the fact that there was someone standing right next to me. So I turned to Kathy and whispered, "I think there's someone standing here next to me."

She replied, "I don't know how to tell you this, but there's a guy standing next to you holding a note in front of your face for you to read."

This was the last thing in the world that I needed as I was preparing to try to raise 14,000 state government workers from the dead.

I asked Kathy what the note said, and she replied, "The note reads *I am deaf. Can you please help me locate the front desk?*"

Without thinking, I turned to the deaf gentleman and replied, "No sir. I am blind, and I can't help you find anything. You're on your own."

I asked Kathy what he was doing now, and she let me know he was holding the note closer. So I explained it to him even louder, but we never did get together on that thing. Somewhere there is a poor deaf man wandering around looking for the front desk, and if you run across him, I hope you will help him.

More importantly and seriously, I hope you will take the potentially most difficult, absurd, or most tragic events in your life and somehow learn to laugh at them. Bad things do happen to good people. Sometimes we don't have a choice about what happens to us, but we always have a choice in what we're going to do about it.

When in doubt, laugh.

Our scrapbooks can provide an instantaneous and overwhelming real-life example of optimism. If you are having trouble feeling positive at any given moment, you can go back to a time and place when you were strong, victorious, triumphant, or just laughed at yourself.

CHAPTER EIGHT

GRATITUDE, FORGIVENESS, AND PRODUCTIVITY

"Optimism is the faith that leads to achievement; nothing can be done without hope."
—HELEN KELLER

Through my books, movies, syndicated columns, and speaking engagements, I have the privilege of communicating a message of success and optimism with millions of people around the world. Many of those people, as I hope you will do, contact me with questions to share their goals and challenges. Through this process, I have discovered that the biggest reason that most people fail to live optimistically and reach their goals is that they are carrying a huge burden of unforgiveness.

Gandhi is known for saying, "You will not be punished for your unforgiveness. You will be punished by it."

None of us are perfect, and when we fail to forgive those whose imperfections have touched us, we buy in to that pessimistic attitude that life isn't fair. When we go through life trying to do our best and others treat us badly, we must forgive them or we will carry that image and bitterness with us making it impossible to feel optimistic about the future.

Psychologists tell us that we all move toward our most dominant thought. This is why enlightened parents avoid the phrase "Don't spill your milk," because it leaves the dominant thought of spilling your milk. Successful football coaches have learned to no longer say, "Don't fumble the football" as it leaves a dominant thought of fumbling the football. If you carry around bitterness and unforgiveness as you remember what someone else did to you in the past, it is impossible to move forward with optimism as you are firmly establishing a dominant thought of unfairness, creating an expectation going forward that will cause you to look for that same outcome in every situation.

Our performance never exceeds our expectations, and we always find what we're looking for.

One of my speaking colleagues got in the habit of calling his aunt whenever he was giving a speech in her hometown of Detroit. He repeatedly invited her to the venue where he was speaking, but while she always seemed glad to hear from him, she never attended one of his speeches. Finally, he asked her why she never came to hear him speak, and she responded in a matter-of-fact way, "There's no parking downtown."

He was puzzled and inquired, "What do you mean there's no parking downtown? There are thousands of cars down here."

She confidently responded, "That's why there's never any parking, because somebody always has all the spaces. Every time I go down there, I look and look but never find any parking."

My colleague's aunt can teach us an important lesson. Just as if you go downtown looking for no parking, you will find there is nowhere to park; and if you carry around bitterness and unforgiveness, you will find that people you meet today will treat you poorly in much the same way that the person from your past whom you won't forgive treated you. Forgiveness is a great way to start each day of the rest of your life with a clean slate and an optimistic outlook. After we forgive others, we need to wish them well and hope they live a successful, optimistic life.

A great litmus test to determine whether we are living optimistically or pessimistically is how we view abundance. Optimists believe that the universe is infinite and that there is more than enough success and happiness for everyone. Pessimists believe that if someone else is successful, happy, or wealthy, it diminishes their own potential.

Imagine you have a friend or a colleague who receives a lucrative raise or bonus. Do you genuinely congratulate them and view their success as confirmation you can be successful, too, or do you secretly think *I don't know why they got a raise or bonus when I work harder than they do, and no one is recognizing my effort. I guess they're just lucky.*

Imagine you have a friend or relative who receives an instant, unexpected windfall by inheriting a fortune or winning the lottery. Are you happy for them and everything they will be able to do with their newfound wealth, or do you secretly resent them lamenting that it should have been you instead of them?

Philanthropy, charity, and volunteering are all great signs of optimism. If we're giving away our time and money to good causes, we are confirming our mindset that we have more than enough, the universe is limitless, and our future is filled with optimism. Optimists are generous givers, and pessimists are reluctant givers or, quite often, takers.

An instant signal as to whether someone you just met is an optimist or pessimist is whether they bring energy and excitement to the room or whether they bring gloom and doom. There are certain people we have all met who seem to energize us. The more time we spend with them, the better we feel. These are optimists. On the other hand, after spending a brief time with a pessimist, you will feel depressed, downcast, and may want to take a nap.

If you're going to live the optimistic life, you need to surround yourself with people who make deposits into your emotional bank and avoid people who constantly make withdrawals. One of the great ironies in life is that optimists give everyone around them a boost in energy and excitement without diminishing their own emotional resources. Pessimists, on the other hand, can pull everyone down to their level.

I met a gentleman on a flight years ago who has become my mental poster child for pessimists. On that particular day, I got on the plane, found my seat, and stowed my carry-on luggage. Not a bad start for a blind guy as a lot can go wrong in that process I'll tell you about another time.

A gentleman sat down next to me, sighing as if he were frustrated and then groaned as if he were in great pain. I stuck out my hand and introduced myself. He offered a weak handshake and mumbled something I couldn't hear that must have been his name.

Then he said, "I hate this airline, my seat's not comfortable, I don't like this city, the airport we will be connecting through, or our final destination." I suspected he didn't like me either, but we didn't get that far into the conversation.

If you fly a lot, you know that there are really only two kinds of flights: The headset flight and the conversation flight. The choice is generally made by your seatmate. I knew after meeting the gentleman seated next to me that I was going to have a headset flight that day. In fact, on that occasion, I invented a third category hereafter known as the high-volume headset flight as I didn't even want any leakage coming through to me from the world-class pessimist I was sitting beside.

A few minutes after takeoff, our flight attendant, who was a nice young lady, came down the aisle and addressed me and the pessimism poster child beside me. She politely said, "Gentlemen, we're going to be serving your dinner in a few moments. Would you prefer the chicken or the beef?"

I responded, "I believe I'll have the chicken today. Thank you."

Then she turned to the pessimism poster child, inquiring, "And sir, could I bring you the chicken or the beef?"

He mumbled, "It doesn't matter."

The flight attendant seemed a bit perplexed but then tried again, asking, "Well, sir, we have plenty of both the chicken and the beef onboard today, so which would you prefer?"

He barked, "It doesn't matter."

Finally, she imploringly explained, "Sir, you are a first-class passenger here on our airline, and it's my job to give you extraordinary service, so could I bring you the chicken or the beef?"

He rudely shouted, "It doesn't matter. Just get out of here and bring me something."

I thought that he was one of those guys who could brighten up a whole room just by leaving.

I resumed listening to my headset to avoid any more of his pessimistic proclamations until the flight attendant returned with our meals. She politely and profession-ally served me the chicken dinner, for which I gratefully thanked her, and then she served the pessimistic passenger next to me the beef dinner. We ate in silence until he began a monologue that lasted throughout most of the rest of the flight explaining what was wrong with the beef dinner and why he wished he had the chicken dinner.

As I got off of that flight and parted company with the gentleman who will forever be my image for all things pessimistic, I realized that's the way most people live their lives. There are a few optimistic people who make the right decisions, and they are the healthy, wealthy, and happy people who get whatever their own definition of success is out of this life. There are a few people who make the wrong decisions who live in prisons and rehab centers, and then there are the vast majority of people who are pessi-mists and never really make a decision at all. Pessimists live with whatever is left over after optimists choose how they want to live this life.

Always remember that not making a decision is a decision.

Gratitude is the antidote for all pessimism. This life lesson was indelibly planted in my mind and spirit by my grandmother.

When I was a young preschool-aged child, my sister was diagnosed with leukemia, and my parents had to take her to various hospitals and treatment centers around the country. This meant I had to spend a lot of time in another state living with my grandparents. I loved my grandparents, but my friends, toys, and dog were back at our home, and I guess I was quite bored at my grandparents' house.

On one fateful day, I guess I was complaining incessantly about my plight, and my grandmother explained, "You can complain all you want to here in our home as soon as you've filled out your Golden List, but we don't allow any complaining from people who don't have a Golden List."

I was baffled and asked, "What's a Golden List?"

Her answer changed my life and the lives of countless people around the world who have learned about the Golden List through my books, movies, columns, and speeches. The Golden List is the surest way I know to live life optimistically. It's quite simple.

Each morning, you take a few moments and list 10 things you are thankful for. That's all you have to do, but its results are profound.

It's the perfect point in this book to express my thanks to Dave Wildasin and his colleagues at Sound Wisdom Publishing without whom you and I would have never connected in this exploration of optimism.

I defy you to list 10 things for which you are thankful and then have a bad day. If at any time you feel you are slipping toward pessimism, just revisit your Golden List prepared that morning and you will be re-energized with optimism. Without realizing it, my grandmother utilized some fairly advanced psychological techniques including immediacy and dominant thoughts as she developed the Golden List.

I get more positive feedback about the Golden List than anything else I have ever written or talked about. An ongoing list of things you are grateful for will remind you that events in the past have culminated to bring you a lot of wonderful things in the present moment. This realization will cause you to feel optimistic about your future.

If you will apply that optimism in your personal and professional life, you will begin to live out your dreams.

Productivity is an important element of sustaining optimism. You may have noticed that on days you get a lot of good work done that creates value for people around you, you feel energized; but on days you do nothing at all or your efforts do not produce anything meaningful, you feel tired and irritated.

Being productive is nothing more than efficiently accomplishing today's portion of our life's mission.

I dedicated an entire book to this topic entitled *The Art of Productivity*. It is a "how to" manual for optimists who are ready to move toward their destiny.

Today is all you have to invest in your future. If you're going to succeed, you're going to do so by optimistically employing the productivity elements of motivation, communication, and implementation. Everyone who has ever succeeded has done so with these principles whether or not they defined them in the terms that you and I are defining them.

Motivation is the fuel that makes your mission toward your personal success possible. Motivation is the first thing we get when we come into this life and the last thing that slips away as we leave. We do everything we do—good or bad—because, for one reason or another, we are motivated to do so. Recognizing that today is the only thing you have to invest toward your success, if you haven't been investing wisely, you have to change your motivation.

Communication is the way you define and share your mission and personal success for yourself and those around you. No one has ever succeeded by themselves. If someone tells you they have never failed at anything, you can confidently let them know that, if nothing else, at a minimum they have failed to recognize the contribution of others.

Unless you can communicate your goals, you really don't own them, and you haven't firmly established them in your own mind. Great educators will tell you that the best way to learn a subject is to teach it. The very process of communicating a lesson drives it deeper into your mind and into your soul.

You will need to build a success team. They cannot draw on your passion. They can only draw on what you communicate. What you feel, think, or believe is meaningless unless you can share it. This can only be done through communication.

Implementation is putting your thoughts, dreams, passions, mission, and personal success goals into action. When it's all said and done in our world, there's a lot more said than done. You will not live out your dreams because you meant to act today or because you intended to take the right steps. Your best intentions are meaningless. You will reap the rewards of optimism and productivity.

If you meant to cook dinner but didn't, you will be hungry. If you meant to light the fire but you failed to act, you will be cold. And, just as certainly, if you don't implement your mission on a daily basis, you will fail.

I wish I could give you the blueprint for your own motivation, communication, and implementation; however, these elements are as individual to you as your fingerprints. Fortunately, you hold the keys to these blueprints of your own motivation, communication, and implementation as well as those members of your success team you will be drawing toward you.

You may think you're motivating an associate by drawing attention to their accomplishments in front of a vast audience. In reality, that may be terrifying, demoralizing, and de-motivating to that individual. In this case, your best intentions will be taking you farther away from your intended goal. You may think you're communicating your mission to those around you who have accepted the task of creating optimism and success; however, if you're communicating in English and they all speak French, or if you're communicating in writing and they can't read, you're not going to succeed.

Remember, as a blind person I can't see the words, but I read more than anyone I know via audiobooks. If you were trying to communicate with me but insisted on doing it through black on white, ink on paper, you and I could not succeed.

And, finally, if you are trying to implement yourself or engage those around you in beginning a task, you've got to understand how everyone, collectively, achieves their maximum performance in order to create optimism and productivity.

If you and your team were committed to the task of rebuilding and restoring the Statue of Liberty as was done several years ago, you would have to motivate your team to give their best efforts to preserve this symbol of our freedom and all it means. You would have to communicate your passion for the project and your instructions for everyone involved, but unless you could implement, nothing that had gone before would really matter.

If you and your team decided that you were going to begin working at 6:00 a.m., but then you discovered that the first ferry boat did not run out to the island where the Statue of Liberty is located until 9:00 a.m., you simply couldn't implement.

More people fail due to misguided motivation, chaotic communication, and inappropriate implementation than anything else.

If you would like to discover your own strengths and preferences relating to motivation, communication, and implementation, you, along with any of your family, friends, or colleagues, can log on to www.UltimateProductivity. com and receive your own productivity assessment, free of charge, by using the access code 586404.

Optimism cannot long exist without productivity. Optimism may begin as a passion or as potential, but it must become practical as it creates a new reality for you and everyone around you.

CHAPTER NINE

OPTIMISM AND OPPORTUNITY

*"Few things in the world are more
powerful than a positive push. A smile.
A world of optimism and hope. A 'You
can do it!' when things are tough."*
—RICHARD M. DEVOS

As a young boy, I visited a maritime museum. That museum featured a display of ancient mariners who were among the first to discover and explore distant lands and the globe as we know it today.

On one of the ships, there was an Asian symbol that I was told stood for the word *Crisis*, but its definition was *Opportunity on a dangerous wind*. As you will readily see, my greatest crisis created my greatest opportunity but not until I learned to view the crisis optimistically.

As I was approaching graduating from college, it became readily apparent that while all the corporate recruiters were on campus making offers to my friends and classmates, no one was going to hire this blind former weightlifter. I remember telling my parents that I had decided not to get a job, which are difficult words for any parent to hear, but instead, I was going to start my own business.

My father told me to stop by his office the next day, and he wanted to give me something. I, being young and naïve, thought he wanted to give me a lot of money to start my entrepreneurial career; but when I got to his office the next day, he immediately informed me he wasn't going to give me a penny and if I ever had any financial success in my life, it was going to come from my own efforts and ingenuity. He went on to say that because he had worked his whole career in the nonprofit arena, he had no experience or expertise to share with me, but he would introduce me to the best entrepreneur he knew. That turned out to be a far greater gift than any amount of seed money or capital he could have given me.

My dad introduced me to Lee Braxton. Mr. Braxton had a second-grade education but made $10 million during the Great Depression and had given most of it away and just lived off his investments.

He made me read *Think and Grow Rich* three times, and I didn't learn until long after his death that Mr. Braxton had been best friends with Napoleon Hill and had actually given the eulogy at Hill's funeral.

Lee Braxton was an eternal optimist. I remember the day when he tossed the morning newspaper on the table between us and said, "There's a million dollars on the front page. Find it."

I read every word of the front page and then considered how all the headlines might relate to one another. I struggled to find the synergy between any of the articles, and in frustration admitted to him I couldn't find it.

He pointed to an article in the bottom left corner of the front page announcing that an area bank that was located on a prominent corner in our city was breaking ground on moving their drive-in banking facilities from the main thoroughfare around the corner onto a smaller side street.

Mr. Braxton asked, "Why would they move their drive-in from a more-accessible location to one harder to reach?"

I shrugged and told him I didn't know. He asked if I knew who was president of that bank. I was pleased to be able to tell him the man's name.

Then Mr. Braxton asked, "What does he do besides run that bank?"

I replied, "He's a deacon at his church, serves on several nonprofit boards, is raising his deceased brother's children, and is the head of the State Highway Commission."

Mr. Braxton exclaimed, "Bingo! You've got it."

I was glad to know that I had it, but I couldn't imagine what I had.

He prompted, "Get out a map of the area, and stare at it until you can tell me why the president of that bank who is the State Highway Commissioner would move his drive-in windows to the side street."

After staring at the map as long as my failing, near-blind eyes would allow, I admitted defeat and told him I couldn't see anything there that mattered because the side street dead-ended at the river.

Then Mr. Braxton showed me what it meant to think out of the box and asked, "Well, what's on the other side of the river?"

It was like one of those pictures in a kids' magazine that showed a tree, but if you looked at it long enough, eight presidents' images would appear. All of a sudden, I envisioned a bridge over that river connecting the state highway to a main artery in town via the side street where the bank's drive-in windows were being moved. All of that came to pass and created many great opportunities.

I remember asking Mr. Braxton how he knew there was a million dollars on the front page that day. He gave me the classic, eternal-optimist's answer. "Jim, I knew there was a million dollars on the front page that day because there's a million dollars waiting for someone to discover it in the newspaper every day."

There are no more opportunities available to optimists than pessimists, but optimists look for opportunities while pessimists look for excuses.

All farmers are optimistic. From the time they plant their seeds until they reap the harvest, they know there are countless things that can go wrong and only one positive outcome; but they believe time and the elements are on their side, so they are able to feed the world.

Opportunities come disguised as problems, and my biggest opportunity certainly came to me through my biggest problem.

As you read this book, I know that you're thinking about your goals and your dreams. My greatest hope is that you will say "Yes" to your ultimate destiny and begin to travel a path that will lead you to the greatness that you were created to enjoy.

I do have to warn you about one thing. As soon as you start down that path—having established your goal—a new group of people will enter your life. These people are called "Pessimists."

These self-imposed experts are not the consultants or professionals we look to for help as we reach for our goals. They are, instead, the small-minded individuals who have never done anything in their lives, nor have they even tried. But they can tell you many reasons why your goal will never work and how foolish you are to think you could ever accomplish anything extraordinary.

If you believe these "experts," they become the most powerful people on the earth. They have the ability to destroy the most magnificent and powerful dream. If you don't believe these "experts," they have no power at all, and they will go away and bother someone else.

Shortly after I emerged from my 9- by 12-foot room, I went to a support meeting for blind and visually impaired people. While there, I met a young lady named Kathy Harper who would become a lifelong friend and colleague. I told her about my frustration in no longer being able to enjoy movies and television and how I thought if we could just add an additional soundtrack to conventional programming, it would become accessible for millions of blind and visually impaired people. We didn't know anything about it but recognized that we shared a spark of optimism.

Kathy and I decided to pursue our dream of making movies and television accessible for blind and visually impaired people. Kathy's research told us that there were 13 million blind and visually impaired people just in the United States and many millions more around the world. So we knew there was a great potential market.

The first so-called "expert" I had to deal with was the voice in my own head asking, "If this is such a great idea, how come no one ever thought of it before?"

It is important to realize that every great idea or development that has ever benefited humanity was met with this same pessimistic question. Many people with great ideas and magnificent goals are stopped by their own question before their dream ever sees the light of day.

Kathy and I were determined to create narrated videotapes that would let blind people "hear what they couldn't see." We began working in our own studio. Actually, I use the term "studio" a bit loosely, as it was the basement of a condominium building in downtown Tulsa, Oklahoma, which you may know is not exactly the entertainment capital of the universe.

Underneath the stairs that led into the basement, there was a broom closet. We took the brooms out of the closet and hung boat cushions inside to help soundproof the space. This became our studio.

At that point, I realized that we needed some studio equipment. After calling several manufacturers and telling them we wanted to buy equipment in order to do TV for the blind, I knew that one of our first obstacles was going to be struggling to be taken seriously.

Finally, I found one manufacturer of studio equipment who was at least willing to listen to me. After hearing about our dream of making television possible for blind people, he talked to his manager and called me back.

He said, "Obviously, we would like to sell you a whole lot of expensive equipment, because that's how we make our living. However, we feel it would be embarrassing to our company for you to buy all of this expensive equipment and then find out that your crazy idea won't work. This would leave a blind guy stuck with our brand of equipment, and we feel it would be a bad reflection on our company. So we're going to loan you the equipment you need in order to get started, and as soon as you figure out that your idea won't work, you call us and we'll come and pick up our equipment."

While it wasn't particularly encouraging, we at least had some equipment in our basement studio. We set it up on a portable card table outside the broom closet.

A lot of people talk themselves out of their dreams because of their own feelings of inadequacy. They feel, because they know themselves better than anyone else, that their low self-esteem must be valid. In reality, very few people really get an accurate picture of themselves. When we are faced with the pressure of pursuing our dreams, we mentally highlight our shortcomings and downplay our talents.

Kathy had left her promising career at a law firm and immediately became our production engineer. My background had been as an investment broker and entrepreneur, and I became the narrator. Many people since that time have pointed out to me that an engineer with a background in the law and a narrator with a background in investment banking seems a bit absurd. In retrospect, I would agree;

however, at the time it never occurred to us. When the dream is big enough, the facts don't count.

Kathy did a great job of running equipment—with a lot of help from the manufacturer's technical representative on the 1-800 trouble line. We were trying to perform a task that had never been done before with equipment designed to do something else, so we had a lot of challenges.

Meanwhile, I was having my own struggle in the broom closet, trying to become a narrator. Today, NTN is blessed to have several world-class experienced voice talents, but at that time, I was it.

As you're reading this book, if you're considering a career change, being a narrator is a fairly simple job. All you have to do is watch the TV monitor and read your script. When the corresponding point in the story appears on your monitor, you read the line as written on your script.

Unfortunately, I could not see the monitor or the script. This "minor" detail created endless difficulties. Kathy and I were writing the scripts as we went along and learning on the fly. Today, we are fortunate to have a number of award-winning scriptwriters. These outstanding writers have received the top scriptwriting award from the Writers Foundation of America.

But at that time, I had to go out where Kathy was sitting at the card table trying to operate our borrowed equipment and have her read me my next line. Then I would rush into the broom closet with boat cushions hanging about me and listen to my headset, waiting for the point when it sounded like it was time to deliver my line. This was an inefficient method to say the least.

Kathy and I were both frustrated with our slow progress.

One morning, Kathy told me that as the Chief Engineer, she had come up with a new development that she felt would improve our efficiency. She had taken one of the brooms that we had moved out of the closet when we turned it into the Narrative Television Network International Headquarters and Studios. She had removed the broom from the handle, and she told me, "If you will just sit in the closet and wait, I will stab you in the back with this broomstick when it's time to deliver your next line."

I found myself sitting in a broom closet with boat cushions hanging all about me, listening on a headset, while waiting to get stabbed by a broomstick. I remember asking myself, "I wonder if Ted Turner got started this way?"

I am now proud to say that Ted Turner serves on our Advisory Board, but in all of my exposure to Mr. Turner, he has never mentioned anything about a broom closet, boat cushions, or being stabbed with a broom handle.

Kathy and I eventually completed our first seven television shows.

Then we had to go into a broadcast studio to mix that new narrative soundtrack we had created back onto our master tape so we could hopefully begin duplicating home videos to send to blind and visually impaired people around the country.

I called studio facilities in our area and found what I believed to be the best. I talked to the head of the studio and told him I needed to work with their best engineer, because we had a unique project that had never been attempted before.

He seemed intrigued and told me to be there at 10:00 the next morning, and he would have his best engineer available.

The next morning, Kathy and I got all of our borrowed equipment, cords, and tapes and put them in a large box, and we headed off for the studio. As Kathy was legally blind and I am totally blind, in more ways than one we were the blind leading the blind.

We arrived at the broadcast studio right on time to receive our next lesson in dealing with "experts and optimism."

As Kathy and I walked into the broadcast studio facility, with her leading me as I carried our huge box with all of our borrowed equipment, I realized how ridiculous we must seem to the "experts" in the television industry.

I set down the huge box and was introduced to the head of the studio. He, in turn, introduced me to their chief engineer who I thought sounded a bit skeptical about our entire project.

As I told him what we were trying to accomplish and how we thought we could improve the lives of blind and visually impaired people around the world, he got even more skeptical. Finally, he said, "Jim, I'm an expert. I've been in this business 21 years. I have seen everything and done everything, and I can absolutely tell you beyond a shadow of a doubt that what you want to do will not work. In fact, I'm so certain it won't work, I will not even take that equipment out of the box and try it."

Immediately, I realized that I had reached a fork in the road. It was the classic choice between optimism and pessimism. I could either listen to this "expert" and give up on our dream, or I could try one more time. When faced with this type of dilemma, I can assure you that the right answer is always to try one more time, because when it comes to your dreams, your goals, and your destiny, it is always too soon to quit.

After being totally rejected by the chief engineer, I turned back to the head of the studio and said, "I need to apologize to you. I know I asked to work with your best engineer, and apparently this is him right here, but do you have anybody back there who's maybe a little less expert than this guy?"

A few minutes later, out came a very young man who introduced himself to me. I shared with him what we were trying to accomplish, and I asked him if he felt it could work.

He said, "Look, I am just a college kid trying to earn a few extra bucks for school. If you want to try it, we can wire it up and try."

I shook his hand and said to Kathy, "I think this is the guy we've been looking for."

Second for second and frame for frame, every one of those shows came together then just like they do now, and less than six months later, Kathy and I (blind leading the blind) traveled to New York City where the National Academy of Television Arts and Sciences presented us with an Emmy Award for engineering expertise that has expanded the scope of television.

We have our Emmy Award displayed in the lobby of NTN today. To me, it has never been a testament to our engineering expertise, but it does signify our willingness to optimistically hold on to our dreams; because I know when I have a dream inside of me—just like the one you have inside of you—I am responsible for it, not some arrogant, pessimistic "expert" who wants to tell me it won't work.

The Narrative Television Network has grown into a successful international business that has spawned all my other business activities. NTN has created a whole new industry, and most of primetime network TV and many first-run movies are now accessible to blind and visually impaired people.

It is ironic that the success of NTN created an opportunity for me to speak, which created an opportunity for me to write books, which created an opportunity to have those books turned into movies, which created an opportunity to have those movies narrated so they are accessible to me. Optimism creates an endless circle of opportunity that will not only change your life but change the world.

CHAPTER TEN

YOUR OPTIMISTIC JOURNEY

"Perpetual optimism is a force multiplier."
—COLIN POWELL

A pessimist can give you a thousand reasons not to start a journey and a hundred reasons to quit along the way; but an optimist needs only one reason, which is more than enough to reach his destiny.

A pessimist will look skeptically at the world around him and challenge, "I'll believe it when I see it." An optimist will look at the same view of the world and confidently proclaim, "I'll see it when I believe it."

Belief is all that optimists need to fuel their dream, but I know from my own experience there are times when I don't feel like acting optimistically. My beloved late, great friend Coach John Wooden would often ask a poignant question. "What would you do right now if you were amazing?" He knew that when you don't feel amazing, it's hard to identify with being amazing; but when you put the tiny phrase "If you were…" before amazing, it releases your imagination and all the possibilities.

As you commence your journey of life as an optimist, I know there are times when you will be nearly overwhelmed by pessimists and pessimistic messages. It might be hard in that moment to think of yourself as an optimist, but if you will ask yourself the powerful question, "What would I do right now if I were an optimist?" your path will become clear.

If we don't control our attitude, other people will. My beloved friend and mentor Dr. Robert Schuller was fond of saying, "I'd rather attempt to do something great and fail than attempt to do nothing and succeed."

In optimism terms, I would echo Dr. Schuller's thoughts by saying, "I'd rather be optimistic and risk disappointment than be pessimistic and be proven right."

I married my wife Crystal shortly after we graduated from college. I would have told anybody who asked that I was an entrepreneur, but in reality we were closer to starving, unemployed imposters.

As you start your journey of optimism from where you are to where you want to be, you may be starting from ground zero or even below the ground. Today as a multimillionaire, I tell people that when we started out, we weren't poor because poor people can't get that far in debt. We had to struggle for several years just to reach ground zero before we began climbing the mountain of our goals toward our destiny.

If you find yourself in a similar place, I want to encourage you because when you've got nothing to lose, you've got everything to gain. I would rather have optimism on my side than money, experience, expertise, education, or contacts. With optimism you can get all those other things, but all those other things without optimism are useless.

When we started out, we had a $350 car that I paid too much money for. We lovingly called it the Green Dog, but it was pathetic. The trunk leaked like a screen door, and my best efforts failed to seal the leaks, so I did the next best thing and drilled several holes through the bottom of the trunk so at least the water would eventually run out. Our Green Dog had a myriad of mechanical symptoms, and if it had been in a hospital, it would have been on the critical list.

I had been exposed to the powerful messages of Dr. Denis Waitley during those many months in my 9- by 12-foot room. I heard he was speaking at a meeting in Phoenix, and I knew we had to get there. Optimists are willing to do what other people won't do because they believe in the power of tomorrow.

We took our Green Dog to a local mechanic and asked him his thoughts on driving it the 2,000-mile round trip to Phoenix. He laughed and said, "You've got about as good a chance of getting to Phoenix as you do of getting off my parking lot."

A pessimist would have heard, "You don't have a chance." But as an optimist, I heard, "Give it a try. What do you have to lose?"

The Green Dog made it to Phoenix and back, and I believe Dr. Waitley's message was the beginning of my growth and success.

I remember sleeping in the Green Dog along the side of the road about halfway to Phoenix. We woke up at almost the same moment, and Crystal told me her watch showed it was about 3:00 a.m. I asked her to look up and down the highway and see if there were any other people spending the night in a $350 car in the midst of a 2,000-mile road trip. She laughed and assured me we were alone.

A pessimist would have said to himself, "You're an idiot," but as an optimist I said, "This proves that we are willing to do what other people won't, so it's just a matter of time until we reach all our goals."

I don't think you should ever take advice from anyone who doesn't have what you want, including me. My personal business is my business until I'm asking you to make life decisions based on my advice. Then my business becomes your business.

When I wrote the book *The Millionaire Map*, I did one of the most difficult things I've ever done. I asked Merrill Lynch and Bank of America to certify my wealth excluding my business holdings, my book and movie royalties, and my real estate. They presented me and my readers of that book with a letter certifying that just in cash on hand and negotiable securities, I have in excess of $10 million. You can view that letter at www.TheMillionaireMap.com.

I share this so you will understand that you've never met anyone more broke, scared, or discouraged than I was as a totally blind person in that 9- by 12-foot room I described to you; but with nothing more than the power of optimism, I have gone from there to here. With optimism, you will find your way and everything you need to get you from where you are to where you want to be. Pessimism only offers you a series of excuses that you can share with the rest of the world. But optimism offers you the whole world. Nothing will happen until you get started. If not now, when? And if not you, who?

THE OPTIMIST'S OATH

I choose to be an optimist
Not because it's easy
But because it's worthy of me and
the choice I have been given.
I realize my road may be long,
The journey may be hard,
And my destination seems impossibly far away;
But I know that optimism will lead me home.
I know the world may call me a fool
As they sit on the sidelines and laugh
at my struggling efforts,
But I know there are fellow
optimists along the way
Who have been where I want to go
And will welcome me into their circle of victory.
To my dying breath, I will choose
To be an optimist
Because the creation around me
Deserves to be viewed as a miraculous masterpiece,
And I deserve to take my place
Among the stars.

—JIM STOVALL
2017

ABOUT JIM STOVALL

In spite of blindness, Jim Stovall has been a National Olympic weightlifting champion, a successful investment broker, the president of the Emmy Award-winning Narrative Television Network, and a highly sought-after author and platform speaker. He is the author of 40 books including the bestseller *The Ultimate Gift*, which is now a major motion picture from 20th Century Fox starring James Garner and Abigail Breslin. Five of his other novels have also been made into movies with two more in production.

Steve Forbes, president and CEO of *Forbes* magazine, says, "Jim Stovall is one of the most extraordinary men of our era."

For his work in making television accessible to our nation's 13 million blind and visually impaired people, the President's Committee on Equal Opportunity selected Jim Stovall as the Entrepreneur of the Year. Jim Stovall has been featured in *The Wall Street Journal*, *Forbes* magazine, *USA Today*, and has been seen on *Good Morning America*, *CNN*, and *CBS Evening News*. He was also chosen as the International Humanitarian of the Year, joining Jimmy Carter, Nancy Reagan, and Mother Teresa as recipients of this honor.

Jim Stovall can be reached at 918-627-1000 or Jim@JimStovall.com.